BAD MEDICINE

VOLUME 1: NEW MOON

No.
2012-0125

CENTERS FOR DISEASE CONTROL
MEDICAL EXAMINER'S REPORT

THE DEPARTMENT OF THE CORONER

XAMINER ....

IOLOGIST ....

IG PHYSICIAN .... Dr. Randa

BY: Captain Tony Chiu   DATE

w York Police Department   TIME:

NAME: Matthew Walter Dalton   D.O.B.
RACE   C
ADDRESS   X

NNER/CIRCUMSTANCES OF DEATH

PRIMARY CAUSE: Brain Hemorrhage Interval: 2-3 days
DUE TO: Presence of retrovirus in cerebrospinal fluic
DUE TO: Injection mark on right arm Interval: 3 days
MANNER OF DEATH: Subject experienced rapid swelling cortex and the premotor regions of the which resulte untreated. It is unclear if immediate Negligence. Th brospinal fluid that sxilar to a retrovirus created The decedent was employed as a lab assitant in the The case was handled by Detective Joely Huffman. Ph handled by the New York Coroner's office, indicated severed — it was simply not case was ref ue's e er Tri Carpenter Trials o modify rate brain it recent invis-

eam

Cardiologist? Is that how we're referring to Doctor Horne? How "Keeper of the

Two notes...

One: Invisible head! How awesome is it that I get to use those together in

Two

do fe

hotter

they giv

Direct

Seriou

we're

new haircut

BAD MEDICINE

VOLUME 1: NEW MOON

WRITTEN BY
NUNZIO DEFILIPPIS & CHRISTINA WEIR

ILLUSTRATED BY
CHRISTOPHER MITTEN

COLORED BY
BILL CRABTREE

LETTERED BY
DOUGLAS E. SHERWOOD

EDITED BY
JAMES LUCAS JONES

DESIGNED BY
KEITH WOOD

PUBLISHED BY ONI PRESS, INC.

PUBLISHER
JOE NOZEMACK

EDITOR IN CHIEF
JAMES LUCAS JONES

ART DIRECTOR
KEITH WOOD

OPERATIONS DIRECTOR
GEORGE ROHAC

MARKETING COORDINATOR
TOM SHIMMIN

EDITOR
JILL BEATON

EDITOR
CHARLIE CHU

DIGITAL PREPRESS LEAD
TROY LOOK

ONI PRESS, INC.
1305 SE Martin Luther King Jr. Blvd.
Suite A
Portland, OR 97214
USA

Become our fan on Facebook: facebook.com/onipress
Follow us on Twitter: @onipress
onipress.tumblr.com
onipress.com

First edition: January 2013

ISBN 978-1-62010-081-3

Library of Congress Control Number: 2012908945

10 9 8 7 6 5 4 3 2 1

PRINTED IN CHINA.

BAD MEDICINE

UNSEEN

MAUNA KEA, HAWAII.

FIVE YEARS AGO...

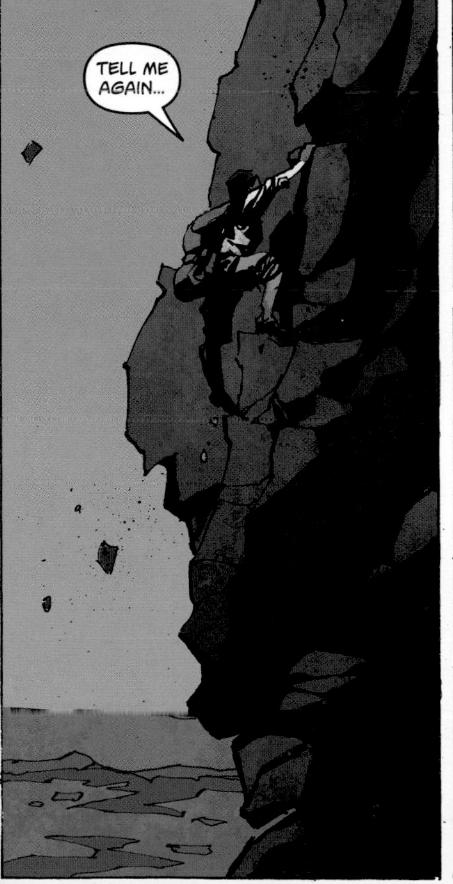

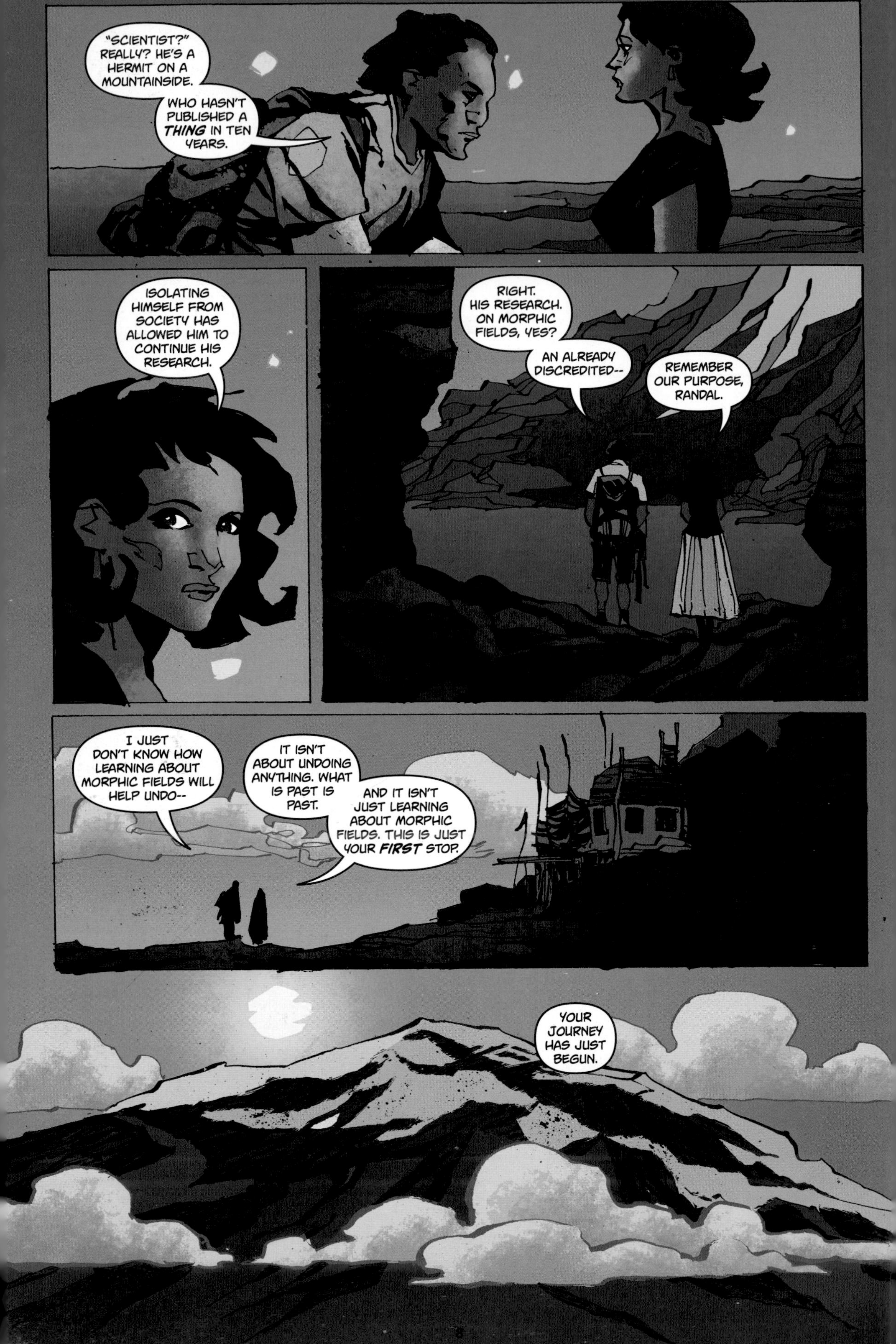

"SCIENTIST?" REALLY? HE'S A HERMIT ON A MOUNTAINSIDE.
WHO HASN'T PUBLISHED A ***THING*** IN TEN YEARS.

ISOLATING HIMSELF FROM SOCIETY HAS ALLOWED HIM TO CONTINUE HIS RESEARCH.

RIGHT. HIS RESEARCH. ON MORPHIC FIELDS, YES?
AN ALREADY DISCREDITED--
REMEMBER OUR PURPOSE, RANDAL.

I JUST DON'T KNOW HOW LEARNING ABOUT MORPHIC FIELDS WILL HELP UNDO--
IT ISN'T ABOUT UNDOING ANYTHING. WHAT IS PAST IS PAST.
AND IT ISN'T JUST LEARNING ABOUT MORPHIC FIELDS. THIS IS JUST YOUR ***FIRST*** STOP.

BROOKLYN, NEW YORK.
TODAY.
WHAT HAVE WE GOT?
LAB IS OWNED BY ONE DOCTOR CHARLES KEEFER, BUT THE DEAD BODY'S I.D. BELONGED TO ONE MATT DALTON. LAB ASSISTANT.
HIS I.D.?
YEAH, WE CAN'T MATCH THE FACE YET, BECAUSE...
...WELL...
...YOU CAN SEE WHY.

WHY IS THERE ALMOST NO *BLOOD?*
YOU GOT ME, DETECTIVE.

SEE IF WE CAN FIND THIS DOCTOR KEEFER. I'LL TAKE A LOOK AT THE BODY.
KNOCK YOURSELF *OUT*.

WHAT THE HELL?
THUD

THAT CAN'T BE RIGHT.

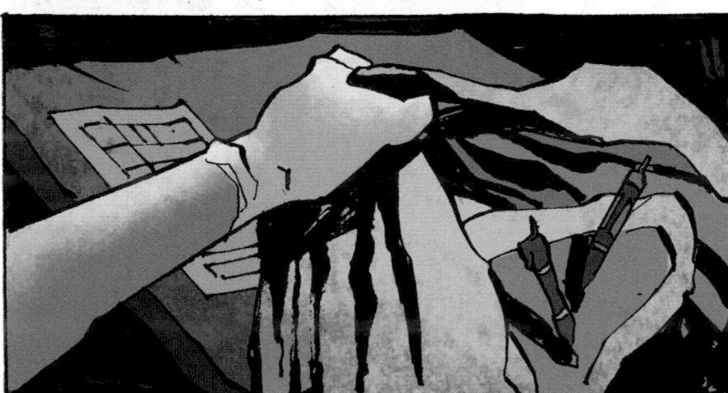

SON OF A BITCH...

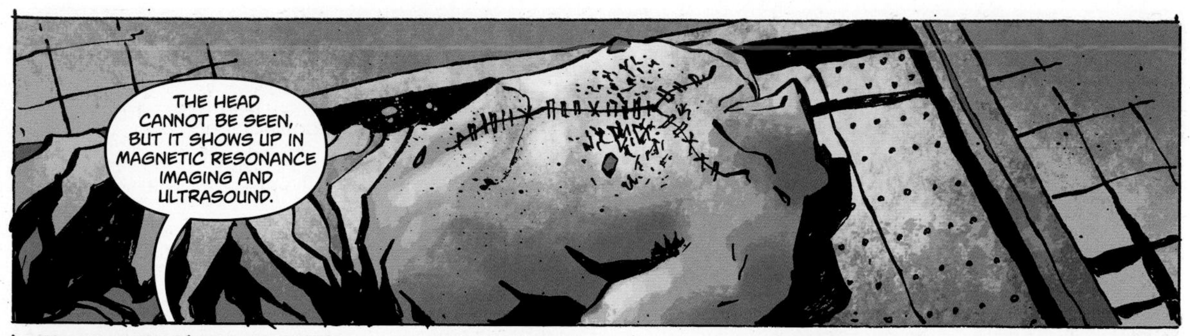
THE HEAD CANNOT BE SEEN, BUT IT SHOWS UP IN MAGNETIC RESONANCE IMAGING AND ULTRASOUND.

BUT WHAT'S THE CAUSE OF DEATH? CLEARLY, *THIS* ISN'T ACTUALLY A WOUND AT ALL.
CAN'T BE SURE. I EXPECT THERE'S SOME SIGN ON THE HEAD ITSELF, SO WHEN WE'VE IMAGED IT AS BEST WE CAN WITH THE TOOLS THAT *DO* WORK, I MAY HAVE ANSWERS.

BUT THERE WAS SOMETHING IN THE *BLOOD*.
A VIRUS, MAYBE A RETROVIRUS.

COULD IT BE A TOXIN? COULD HE HAVE BEEN POISONED?
UNCLEAR. I'VE NEVER SEEN ANYTHING LIKE IT. HELL, IT COULD JUST BE A *DISEASE*.

A DISEASE THAT...?
HEY DON'T LOOK AT ME. I JUST *WORK* HERE.

DETECTIVE HUFFMAN!

ANY PROGRESS ON THE HEADLESS HORSEMAN?

FINGERPRINTS SHOW THE VICTIM WAS IN FACT MATTHEW DALTON, THE LAB ASSISTANT. HE ONCE WORKED IN A FEDERAL RESEARCH FACILITY, SO WE GOT LUCKY HIS PRINTS WERE ON FILE.
NO SIGN OF DOCTOR KEEFER, DALTON'S BOSS.
AND THE M.E. JUST GAVE ME A RUNAROUND ON CAUSE OF DEATH.

YEAH, I SAW HIS PRELIMINARY FINDINGS. I'M CALLING FOR *HELP* ON THIS ONE.
YOU GOTTA GIVE ME--
MISSING HEADS? VIRUSES IN THE SYSTEM? IF THIS *IS* A DISEASE, I WANT SOME BACKUP BEFORE IT *SPREADS*.

IT'S *NOT* A DISEASE. IF ANYTHING, IT'S AN EXPERIMENT GONE WRONG.
BUT KEEFER'S LAB HAD ZERO NOTES ON WHATEVER HE WAS RESEARCHING. THE ONLY THING WE FOUND WAS THIS ONE GUY'S *NAME*.

DOCTOR RANDAL HORNE...?
YEAH. LET ME AT LEAST--
NOPE. I'M NOT WAITING. YOU GO AHEAD AND FIND THIS HORNE.
BUT ME...? I'M CALLING FOR SOME *BACKUP*.

CENTERS FOR DISEASE CONTROL.

DRUID HILLS, GEORGIA.

AN INVISIBLE HEAD? IS THIS A JOKE?

IT'S NOT A JOKE. IT'S A RETROVIRUS.

THE AUTOPSY SHOWED THAT THE CORPSE HAD A RETROVIRUS IN HIS BLOOD. TAKE A LOOK.

DR. MADELEINE DUMONT
DEPUTY DIRECTOR

NEW YORK PRESBYTERIAN HOSPITAL.
WEILL CORNELL MEDICAL CENTER.

DOCTOR RANDAL HORNE...?
THIS IS HIS LAST KNOWN PLACE OF EMPLOYMENT.
SORRY. THAT WAS BEFORE MY TIME.

PERHAPS IF YOU TALKED TO HUMAN RESOURCES...
I DID. I TALKED WITH H.R., AND THE ADMINISTRATION. NO ONE GAVE ME ANYTHING, EXCEPT THAT HE USED TO WORK HERE. IN CARDIOLOGY.
WELL, I'M NOT SURE I'M ABLE TO HELP YOU.

DO YOU SEE THIS BADGE? I'M A DETECTIVE. I WORK HOMICIDE.
THAT MEANS SOMEONE IS DEAD. AND THIS DOCTOR HORNE MAY BE ABLE TO HELP ME FIND OUT WHY.
SO YOU'D BETTER FIND A WAY TO HELP ME OR I'LL HAUL YOUR--

DETECTIVE! DETECTIVE!
I'M DOCTOR JAMES LUCAS... I KNEW RANDAL HORNE.

BEFORE HE WALKED AWAY FROM MEDICINE FIVE YEARS AGO, RANDAL HORNE WAS THE MOST BRILLIANT DOCTOR I'D EVER MET.
AND HE *KNEW* IT.

A GENIUS WITH *ZERO* BEDSIDE MANNER.
UNLESS HE WAS DEALING WITH A REP FROM A PHARMACEUTICAL COMPANY. FOR THEM, HE COULD TURN ON THE CHARM.

SORRY. THERE'S NO SMOKING IN HERE.
I KNOW. NO SMOKING ANYWHERE IN A HOSPITAL.

THEN WHY..? NEVER MIND.

ANY IDEA WHERE HORNE IS NOW?
NOT A CLUE. HE WENT ON SOME WORLDWIDE JOURNEY. PROBABLY TO AVOID LOSING HIS LICENSE TO PRACTICE.
LOSING HIS LICENSE? BUT YOU SAID HE WAS *BRILLIANT*.

HE WAS.
BUT EVEN SO... HE DID *KILL* A PATIENT.

YOU HAVE GOT TO SEE THIS.
OR NOT SEE IT. IT'S CRAZY--THE HEAD, IT'S IN-FRAKKING-VISIBLE.

ARE YOU SURE WE SHOULD BE DOING THIS? I MEAN, I'M NOT SURE I EVEN WANT TO SEE IT. AND WE COULD GET IN TROUBLE. COULDN'T WE?

BERT?

GOTCHA. GOD, KID, YOU'RE EASY TO SCARE.
SO. NOT. FUNNY.

READY?

HEY, MERLIN.

I'M SORRY THIS IS SO LATE. LONG DAY.

STOP IT, YOU LITTLE FREAK.

HSSSSSSS

MERLIN?
SSH. IT'S OKAY, BOY.

YOU'VE REACHED RANDAL HORNE. THE WORLD IS FULL OF MYSTERIES. ONE OF THEM WILL BE SOLVED ONCE YOU LEAVE A MESSAGE.

DR. HORNE...? THIS IS DETECTIVE JOELY HUFFMAN OF THE NEW YORK POLICE DEPARTMENT. YOUR NAME WAS MENTIONED IN THE NOTES OF DR. CHARLES KEEFER.
WE FOUND A **DEAD BODY** IN HIS LAB, AND ANY LIGHT YOU CAN SHED ON HIS WORK WOULD BE OF GREAT HELP...
NYPD

IT'S A VOICE MESSAGE SERVICE. LEFT THE GOOD DOCTOR A VOICEMAIL.
ANY PRINTS?
GOT A PARTIAL. WE'RE RUNNING IT NOW.

LET ME KNOW WHAT COMES BACK, OR IF DOCTOR HORNE CONTACTS YOU.
CAPTAIN...?
BUT FOR NOW...

...WE GOT **BACKUP** FROM THE **C.D.C.**
YO... WHERE DO YOU KEEP THE INVISI-HEAD BODIES AT?

I AM DR. ALEXANDER TEAGUE. I'M A PATHOLOGIST, WHICH MAKES ME AN EXPERT IN COMMUNICABLE DISEASES.
AND NOXIOUS PERSONALITIES.
MY COLLEAGUE IS DR. IAN HOGARTH, FORENSIC SPECIALIST. THERE IS NO ONE BETTER WITH DEAD BODIES.

I'M FLATTERED. AND HERE I THOUGHT YOU HATED ME.
AND HERE I WOULD BE RIGHT.
UNFORTUNATELY, WORKING WITH HIM MEANS LISTENING TO HIM SPEAK.

NICE TO--
I GIVE YOU OUR CREDENTIALS BY WAY OF EXPLAINING WHOSE TIME YOU ARE **WASTING** WITH YOUR JUVENILE PRANK.

EXCUSE ME? PRANK?
PHOTOSHOP MAKES ALTERING IMAGES CHILD'S PLAY.

LET ME GET THIS STRAIGHT:
I BUST MY ASS ALL THE WAY TO DETECTIVE, BUT DECIDE TO RISK IT ALL TO SEND A PHOTOSHOPPED PICTURE OF A CORPSE TO THE FEDS?
AND I DO THIS... WHY? FOR SHITS AND GIGGLES?

AH, DETECTIVE HUFFMAN... YOU'RE HERE! BIG NEWS!
IT SEEMS THE HEAD HAS... **REAPPEARED**.
HOW CONVENIENT.

ANYBODY HUNGRY?

OH, LOOK. DR. HOGARTH IS MAKING A JOKE ABOUT A DEAD BODY. POSITIVELY SHOCKING.
KILLJOY.
YOU TWO ARE CUTE. YOU SHOULD EITHER GET MARRIED OR TAKE THIS ACT ON THE ROAD.

I NEED TO LEAVE SOON. HAVE EITHER OF YOU ACTUALLY FOUND ANYTHING?
THE RETROVIRUS IN THE BLOOD IS A MODIFIED VERSION OF ONE TESTED A FEW YEARS BACK FOR ITS ABILITY TO INCREASE BRAIN CELL PRODUCTION.

SO HOW WOULD THAT CAUSE EITHER THE DEATH, OR THE HEAD'S... DISAPPEARANCE?
THE LATTER? IT WOULDN'T.

BUT THE FORMER... HIS BRAIN SWELLED RAPIDLY, CAUSING SEIZURES, HEMORRHAGE... AND THEN A NICE PERMANENT VACATION ON MY SLAB.

WELL, IT'S A START. I'LL CHECK BACK IN A COUPLE OF HOURS. I GOTTA GO MEET A GUY.
HOT DATE?
THE GUY I'M MEETING, DOC...? NOT EVEN REMOTELY MY TYPE.

ARE YOU NERVOUS?
OF COURSE NOT.

IT **HAS** BEEN SEVERAL YEARS SINCE YOU WERE IN NEW YORK. IT WOULD MAKE SENSE IF YOU FELT--
IT'S NOT MY HOME. IT HASN'T BEEN FOR A LONG TIME.

WHAT ABOUT YOU?

I KNOW YOU'RE NOT VERY ATTACHED TO MATERIAL THINGS...

...BUT DO YOU MISS NEW YORK?
YOU KNOW I DON'T.

DOCTOR RANDAL HORNE...? I'M DETECTIVE JOELY HUFFMAN.

ARE YOU TRAVELING WITH SOMEONE?
NO. I ALWAYS TRAVEL *ALONE*.
THEN WHO WERE YOU TALKING TO..?
AN OLD FRIEND.

NO LUGGAGE?
JUST THIS. I TRAVEL LIGHT.
FAIR ENOUGH.

SO, THIS CASE YOU WANT MY HELP WITH... HAVE YOU FOUND DR. KEEFER YET?
NO, BUT HE LEFT A PARTIAL PRINT ON A NOTE WITH YOUR NUMBER ON IT.
LISTEN... BEFORE WE START... I NEED TO ASK YOU SOMETHING. ABOUT YOUR PAST.

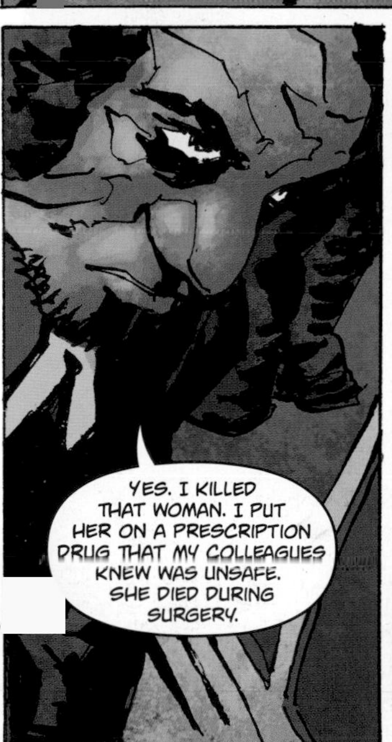
YES. I KILLED THAT WOMAN. I PUT HER ON A PRESCRIPTION DRUG THAT MY COLLEAGUES KNEW WAS UNSAFE. SHE DIED DURING SURGERY.

AND *THAT* IS WHY I ALWAYS TRAVEL *ALONE*.

WHEN DR. CARPENTER TESTED HIS RETROVIRUS SIX YEARS AGO, I WAS BROUGHT IN TO ADDRESS ANY CARDIO CONCERNS.
THEN DR. KEEFER CONTACTED ME TWO YEARS AGO. AND I GAVE HIM INFORMATION ABOUT THE CARPENTER TRIALS.

DIDN'T YOU SIGN AN N.D.A. LIKE EVERY OTHER DOCTOR INVOLVED IN THE CARPENTER TRIALS?
I DON'T RECALL YOU BEING IN ON THOSE TRIALS, DR... TEAGUE, WAS IT? HOW DID YOU RECOGNIZE THE RETROVIRUS IF THE N.D.A.S WERE SO SACROSANCT?

OH, SPEECHLESS. YOU'RE THE ONLY ONE WHO'S EVER BEEN ABLE TO DO THAT TO HIM. I LIKE YOU ALREADY.
WHEN YOU MET WITH DR. KEEFER, WAS HE WORKING ON ANYTHING THAT WOULD EXPLAIN THIS?

HE MADE IT WORK.

HE MADE IT WORK.
MADE WHAT WORK?

MIND OVER MATTER.

BULLSHIT. INVISIBLE HEADS? MIND OVER MATTER? IS THIS A CRIMINAL INVESTIGATION OR A MAGIC ACT?
I VOTE FOR BOTH. I'D PAY FOR THAT SHIT.
DETECTIVE, THIS IS NONSENSE. HE SHOULDN'T EVEN BE HERE.
HE NEARLY LOST HIS MEDICAL LICENSE AND HAS BEEN ON SOME SORT OF FIVE YEAR WALKABOUT SINCE.
HIS ONLY RECENT CONTACT WITH THE MEDICAL COMMUNITY HAS BEEN TO PROVIDE DR. KEEFER WITH A RETROVIRUS THAT *KILLED* HIS ASSISTANT.
WHAT DOES THAT BRING YOUR BODY COUNT TO, "DOCTOR"?
TWO. I'VE LOST PLENTY OF PATIENTS, BUT THERE HAVE BEEN EXACTLY *TWO* PEOPLE WHOSE DEATH *I* CAUSED.
UNTIL YOUR PHONE CALL, I'D BELIEVED THAT COUNT WAS *ONE*.
I TAKE FULL RESPONSIBILITY. AND DETECTIVE, I'M NOT GOING ANYWHERE UNTIL I HELP YOU SOLVE THIS.
NOT TO RAIN ON YOUR REDEMPTIVE PARADE OR ANYTHING, BUT WHERE'S THE MYSTERY? DOCTOR TAMPERS WITH RETROVIRUS, TESTS IT ON HIS ASSISTANT, ASSISTANT DIES. CASE CLOSED.
JUST ARREST THE GUY, RIGHT?
THERE'S YOUR PROBLEM. YOU'RE NOT GOING TO BE ABLE TO ARREST DR. KEEFER. YOU WON'T FIND HIM ANY MORE THAN YOU COULD FIND THAT HEAD.
ARE YOU SAYING DR. KEEFER IS INVISIBLE?

SURE. WHY NOT? HE CAN ALSO FLY AND SHOOT FIRE BEAMS FROM HIS ASS.
I TOTALLY THOUGHT YOU'D GO WITH FIRE FROM HIS EYES. BUT KUDOS TO YOU. WAY MORE *VIVID* THIS WAY!

WHEN I WAS DOING MY "WALKABOUT", I WAS INVESTIGATING THINGS MODERN MEDICINE AND SCIENCE DEEM IMPOSSIBLE. I HELPED DR. KEEFER BECAUSE WHAT HE WAS TRYING TO DO FELL IN THAT CATEGORY.
IN 2007, PROFESSOR GARRET MODDEL TESTED THE CAPACITY OF A GROUP OF STUDENTS TO "BEND LIGHT." THESE STUDENTS WERE ABLE TO CHANGE THE AMOUNT OF REFLECTED LIGHT IN A CONTROLLED EXPERIMENT BY .05%.

AN UNSUPPORTABLE EXPERIMENT YIELDING INSIGNIFICANT RESULTS.
A ***DUPLICATED*** EXPERIMENT YIELDING MINOR BUT STATISTICALLY SIGNIFICANT RESULTS.

DR. KEEFER REPLICATED THE RESULTS, AND MONITORED WHICH SECTIONS OF THE BRAIN WERE ACTIVE FOR THESE MIND-OVER-LIGHT EFFORTS.
THOSE WERE THE AREAS OF THE BRAIN HE TARGETED WITH HIS DOCTORED RETROVIRUS.

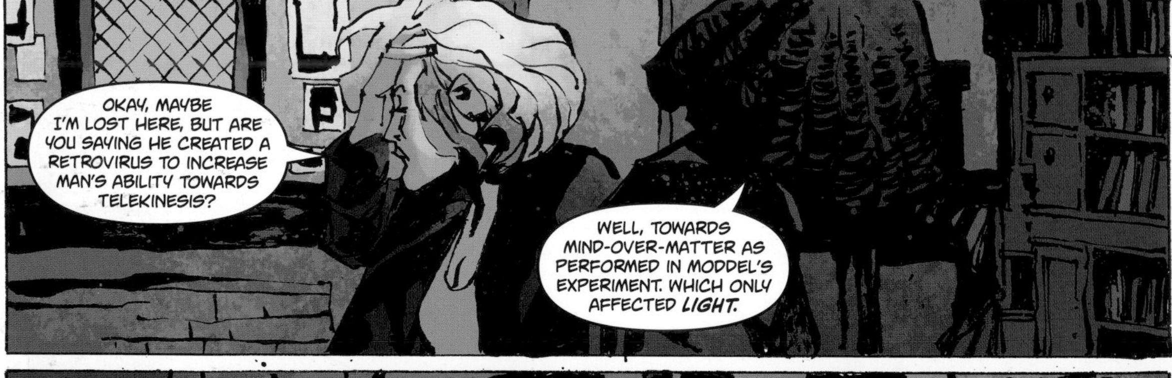
OKAY, MAYBE I'M LOST HERE, BUT ARE YOU SAYING HE CREATED A RETROVIRUS TO INCREASE MAN'S ABILITY TOWARDS TELEKINESIS?
WELL, TOWARDS MIND-OVER-MATTER AS PERFORMED IN MODDEL'S EXPERIMENT. WHICH ONLY AFFECTED ***LIGHT***.

BUT HE MODIFIED IT INCORRECTLY. THE TISSUE GREW OUT OF CONTROL AND KILLED HIS ASSISTANT.

ONE BIG HOLE IN YOUR THEORY. WE HAVE TO ASSUME IT WORKED IN ORDER TO EXPLAIN THE INVISIBLE HEAD. BUT WE HAVE TO ASSUME IT FAILED IN ORDER TO EXPLAIN THE DEAD ASSISTANT.
THOSE TWO ASSUMPTIONS CAN'T BOTH BE CORRECT.

THEY CAN IF HE EXPERIMENTED TWICE. ONCE ON DALTON, AND ONCE ON HIMSELF.
BUT IF IT FAILED WITH DALTON...
THEN THERE WAS NOTHING INHERENT IN DALTON TO MAKE HIS HEAD INVISIBLE. SOMEONE ELSE WAS BENDING LIGHT AROUND DALTON'S HEAD.

THE SON OF A BITCH STAYED WITH THE BODY...
...UNTIL HE CAME TO MY APARTMENT, AT WHICH POINT THE HEAD BECAME VISIBLE BACK IN THE LAB.

YOU HAD AN INVISIBLE GUY IN YOUR APARTMENT? KINKY!
I MEAN, CREEPY.
WHY WOULD HE DO ALL OF THIS?
BECAUSE HE NEEDED US TO KNOW HE'D SUCCEEDED.
THEN WHY COULDN'T WE FIND ANY OF HIS RESEARCH NOTES?

BECAUSE... HE NEEDED ME TO KNOW.

AM I CORRECT, DR. KEEFER?

OOF!

I... THIS ISN'T POSSIBLE.

RELEASE DR. TEAGUE *NOW*, KEEFER.

Brooklyn, New York.

72nd Police Precinct.

HE PUSHED ME. HE PUSHED ME! THAT LUNATIC TOOK ME OUT A WINDOW!
JUST A FEW BRUISES AND SCRAPES. WE'LL HAVE YOU CLEANED UP AND OUT OF HERE IN NO TIME.
MAN, YOU WERE CRAZY LUCKY THAT DUMPSTER WAS THERE.

I'M NOT ENTIRELY SURE IT WAS LUCK. I THINK KEEFER CAREFULLY ORCHESTRATED THE WHOLE SCENE.
IT'S A GREAT WAY TO MAKE A DRAMATIC DISPLAY AND NO ONE GETS HURT.

GREAT. SO HE'S A CONSIDERATE LUNATIC.
YOU CAN BE DAMN SURE THIS GOES ON HIS LIST OF CRIMES.
YOU KNOW, UH, TECHNICALLY, NO ONE SAW HIM PUSH YOU.

I KNOW IT SOUNDS STRANGE, CAPTAIN, BUT THERE WAS NO ONE THERE.
SIR, I'M A TRAINED DETECTIVE. IF THERE WAS SOMETHING TO SEE, I'D HAVE SEEN IT.
I HAVE ZERO PATIENCE RIGHT NOW FOR FAIRY TALES ABOUT INVISIBLE MEN.

SERIOUSLY? COME ON! ONE OF YOU HAD TO CATCH A GLIMPSE OF HIM.
NOPE. DEAD SERIOUS. I PROMISE YOU.
YOU'RE ALL DONE, SIR.

DAMN RIGHT I'M DONE. I'M OUT OF HERE.

WEREN'T YOU THE ONE WHO TOLD ME I NEEDED TO OPEN MY EYES AND ACTUALLY SEE THE WORLD AROUND ME?
IMAGINE THAT... TAKING MY ADVICE.
ONCE UPON A TIME I NEVER WOULD HAVE BELIEVED WHAT KEEFER ACHIEVED WAS POSSIBLE.
SO BY OPENING YOUR EYES, YOU HAVE SEEN THE *UNSEEN*.
ARE YOU KIDDING ME...?
YOU ALWAYS WERE A SUCKER FOR A PRETTY VIEW.
HEADLESS BODIES? INVISIBLE MEN? THIS IS *AWESOME*.
AWESOME IS ONE WORD FOR IT.
LOOK DETECTIVE, DON'T YOU WORRY. TEAGUE MAY HAVE RABBITED, BUT I'M HERE FOR YOU. I PROMISE YOU, WHATEVER HAPPENS, I'M IN IT FOR THE LONG HAUL.
LUCKY...
...ME.

I'M NOT SURE WHAT TO DO NEXT. CLEARLY HE WANTED TO GET OUR ATTENTION.
HEY!

DETECTIVE? WHAT CAN I DO FOR YOU?
IS THAT YOU, KEEFER?

NO. I'M JUST TALKING WITH REBECCA.
REBECCA... MORGAN?
YES. THE WOMAN I KILLED. IT HELPS ME CLEAR MY HEAD.

LOOK, DOCTOR... IN A CASE WITH AN *INVISIBLE* MURDER SUSPECT, IT LOOKS A LITTLE *SUSPICIOUS* IF YOU GO AROUND TALKING TO NO ONE.
I KNOW. THAT'S WHY I CAME OUT HERE TO DO IT *ALONE*.

FINE. DO WHAT YOU HAVE TO DO. BUT WE HAVE A MURDER SUSPECT TO APPREHEND SO COME BACK INSIDE ONCE YOU'RE SORTED.

DR. HORNE... IT'S BEEN A WHILE.

A LOT OF PEOPLE ARE LOOKING FOR YOU, DR. KEEFER.
YOU HEARD THE DETECTIVE. THEY THINK I'M A MURDER SUSPECT.

I'M A SCIENTIST. IT'S ABOUT LOOKING TO THE FUTURE. WHAT HAPPENED TO MATT WAS A TRAGEDY. BUT IT WASN'T INTENTIONAL.
NO GREAT ADVANCE HAS COME WITHOUT A PRICE. BUT IT'S THE BRAVE... THE BOLD WHO KEEP PUSHING FORWARD.

DR. KEEFER! YOU NEED TO COME WITH ME.
EVERYONE JUST STAY CALM.
FUCK *CALM*. YOU *LIED* TO ME.

SORRY, DETECTIVE. I'M *NOT* GOING TO TURN MY-SELF IN.

SHIT--!

I WON'T BE PUNISHED WHEN I DID *NOTHING* WRONG!
SPLASH

I ASSURE YOU, HE *JUST* ARRIVED. I REALLY *WAS* TALKING WITH REBECCA BEFORE.

DR. KEEFER WILL HAVE TO BE HANDLED... DELICATELY. HE HAS A CERTAIN *ARROGANCE* THAT WON'T LET HIM BACK DOWN.
LET'S JUST SAY I RECOGNIZE THAT ARROGANCE.

CENTERS FOR DISEASE CONTROL.
I'VE READ YOUR REPORT, DR. TEAGUE.
I KNOW IT MUST READ LIKE SCIENCE FICTION BUT--
WE'RE INTERESTED IN OFFERING DR. KEEFER A DEAL.

YOU HAVE GOT TO BE KIDDING ME. THIS GUY IS A CRACKPOT. NO WAY HE CAN BE INVISIBLE.
DID YOU OR DID YOU NOT SAY THE WITNESSES REPORTED SEEING NO ONE PUSH YOU OUT A WINDOW?
WELL, THAT'S WHAT THEY SAID...

CERTAIN GOVERNMENT OFFICIALS BELIEVE WE COULD BENEFIT GREATLY FROM FURTHER RESEARCH. CLEARLY WHAT WAS STARTED WITH THE CARPENTER TRIALS HAS EVOLVED INTO SOMETHING... GREATER.

I'VE BEEN AUTHORIZED TO TALK TO THE D.A.'S OFFICE AND MAKE SURE THIS IS CLASSIFIED AS A LAB ACCIDENT AND NOT MURDER.
YOU WILL DELIVER THE OFFER TO KEEFER.

YES, MA'AM.

WE CAN KEEP SEARCHING, BUT HE WON'T BE *FOUND*. HE DOESN'T THINK HE DID ANYTHING WRONG.

I DON'T CARE WHAT HE THINKS. THERE WAS A MURDER. THE MURDER HAPPENED IN HIS LAB AS A RESULT OF HIS "EXPERIMENTS." THAT MEANS HE GETS HIS ASS IN HERE AND ANSWERS MY QUESTIONS.

CHANGE IN PLANS. THE D.A. IS GOING TO OFFER HIM A DEAL.

WHAT???

THEY SAY IT WAS "ACCIDENTAL" AND WANT TO SET HIM UP IN A RESEARCH LAB. DR. TEAGUE'S RETURNING WITH THE OFFICIAL OFFER.

CAPTAIN CHIU, IF POSSIBLE I'D LIKE TO ACCOMPANY WHOEVER IS GOING TO PRESENT THE DEAL TO HIM.
THIS ARRANGEMENT IS BEING HANDLED BY THE C.D.C. YOU'RE FREE TO TALK TO TEAGUE ABOUT WHATEVER YOU WANT.

IS EVERYONE HERE FUCKING NUTS? A MAN IS *DEAD!*

WATCH YOUR TONE, DETECTIVE HUFFMAN. THE SOONER THIS CASE IS OFF MY DESK, THE HAPPIER I WILL BE. UNDERSTAND?
OH, I'LL GET THE DAMN CASE OFF YOUR DESK, SIR. *BEFORE* THAT OFFER COMES IN.

SOUNDS LIKE SHE WAS PISSED. WISH I'D SEEN THAT.
WHAT? I BET SHE'S PRETTY AWESOME WHEN SHE'S ANGRY.

OKAY, DOCTOR TEAGUE. YOU'RE ON.
TALKING TO AN EMPTY LAB. I FEEL LIKE A JACKASS.
MAKES YOU FEEL ANY BETTER, YOU'RE ABOUT TO LOOK LIKE ONE, TOO.

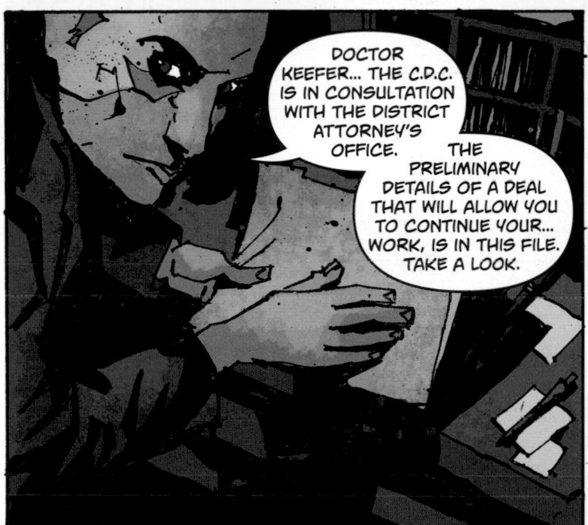
DOCTOR KEEFER... THE C.D.C. IS IN CONSULTATION WITH THE DISTRICT ATTORNEY'S OFFICE.
THE PRELIMINARY DETAILS OF A DEAL THAT WILL ALLOW YOU TO CONTINUE YOUR... WORK, IS IN THIS FILE. TAKE A LOOK.

CHARLES... IF YOU'RE HERE... I URGE YOU TO CONSIDER THIS OFFER AND CONTACT DOCTOR TEAGUE.

I HOPE HE TAKES THE DEAL. I'D LOVE TO ASK HIM SOME QUESTIONS ABOUT HIS FINDINGS.
HE'D BE AN *IDIOT* NOT TO. THOUGH I SUSPECT *WE'RE* THE IDIOTS HERE.
I UNDERSTAND HOW EASY IT IS TO DISMISS THE UNEXPLAINABLE, DR. TEAGUE. IT HAS TAKEN ME *MANY* YEARS TO ACCEPT THAT THERE ARE A VAST NUMBER OF SCIENCES WE HAVE YET TO PUT A NAME TO.
SPARE ME YOUR HIPPIE-NEW-AGE-I'VE-FOUND-GOD RHETORIC. I'M SIMPLY CARRYING OUT THE ORDERS OF THE HIGHER UPS AT THE C.D.C. THEY THINK THIS IS WORTH EXPLORING.
WE'RE WASTING OUR TIME. HE HASN'T BEEN HOME IN WEEKS.
I SINCERELY WISH YOU'D BE HIT BY A CAR RIGHT NOW.
NO. HE HASN'T BEEN *SEEN* AT HOME IN WEEKS. BIG DIFFERENCE.
WE'VE LEFT A COPY OF THE DEAL EVERYWHERE HE MIGHT FIND IT. NOW WE LET HIM FIND US.

NEW YORK PRESBYTERIAN HOSPITAL.
WHAT ARE YOU DOING HERE?

I CAME TO SEE YOU.
YOUR CHANCES FOR SUCCESS WOULD HAVE BEEN GREATER IF YOU'D COME INSIDE.

THERE'S NO JOB FOR YOU HERE.

I DIDN'T COME LOOKING FOR A JOB.

OH...

SO, HOW'RE YOU DOING? YOU KNOW... SINCE... WELL, SINCE...
BETTER.
THAT'S GOOD TO HEAR.

REBECCA KEEPS ME CENTERED. KEEPS ME FROM KILLING MYSELF.
WHAT?

SHE'S BEEN AMAZING. REALLY OPENED MY EYES. SHE'S GOTTEN ME TO BE RECEPTIVE TO ALL SORTS OF NEW THEORIES AND IDEAS. THERE IS SCIENCE OUT THERE THAT WE'VE NEVER DREAMED OF.

I'M SURE THERE IS, BUT YOU'RE STILL MISSING THE POINT.
WE'RE DOCTORS. AND MEDICINE AT ITS BEST IS ABOUT PEOPLE. YOU NEVER SAW THE PEOPLE, RANDAL. STILL DON'T.
AND THAT'S WHY THERE'S NO JOB HERE FOR YOU.

BUT I AM GLAD YOU'RE DOING BETTER. TAKE CARE OF YOURSELF.

HEY. I NEED YOU TO DO SOMETHING FOR ME.

I DON'T UNDERSTAND WHAT YOU'RE ASKING ME HERE. I ALREADY EXPLAINED MY FINDINGS.
BUT I WANT TO KNOW ABOUT THE MAN, NOT THE SCIENCE.
WHATEVER THE HELL THAT MEANS.

YOU SAID THE RAPID CELL GROWTH CAUSED PARTS OF THE BRAIN TO PRESS UP AGAINST THE SKULL. WHICH PARTS?
AND WHAT WOULD IT DO TO YOUR PERSONALITY IF YOU SURVIVED?

OH... I GET IT. YEAH, OKAY, THE PRESSURE WAS ON THE FRONTAL LOBE.
BEEN A WHILE SINCE MED SCHOOL, BUT THAT'S THE PART OF THE BRAIN THAT CAN RECOGNIZE FUTURE CONSEQUENCES FROM CURRENT ACTIONS, HELPING US CHOOSE BETWEEN GOOD AND BAD ACTIONS, YES?

YEP. ALSO PLAYS A ROLE IN LONGER TERM MEMORIES AND SOCIAL NORMS.

SO... EVEN IF IT'S NOT FATAL, THE LINE BETWEEN GOOD AND BAD GETS BLURRED. AND SOCIAL NORMS AND CONSEQUENCES CEASE TO MATTER.
WELL, SURE, THAT'S POSSIBLE...

OH, THAT WOULD BE BAD.

SOMEONE NEEDS TO LET TEAGUE KNOW. MAYBE WE CAN TAKE BACK THE OFFER.

THIS IS A **SERIOUS** HYPOTHESIS YOU'RE MAKING.
VERY.

THEN IF KEEFER IS ALLOWED TO CONTINUE HIS EXPERIMENTS...
...HIS CONDITION ALL BUT GUARANTEES HE WON'T FOLLOW ANY ETHICAL GUIDELINES. THAT'S WHY WE HAVE TO CALL **OFF** THE DEAL.

OOF...

WHAT THE--

KEEFER...?

WHAT DO YOU THINK?

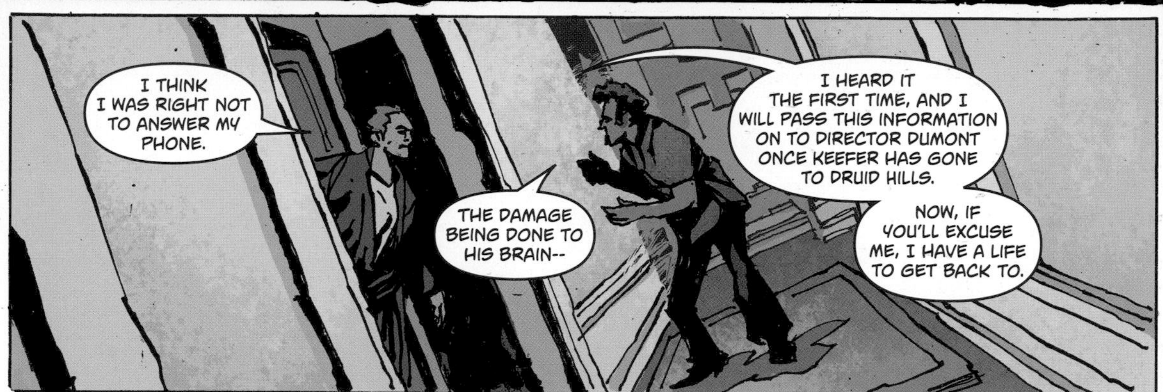
I THINK I WAS RIGHT NOT TO ANSWER MY PHONE.
THE DAMAGE BEING DONE TO HIS BRAIN--
I HEARD IT THE FIRST TIME, AND I WILL PASS THIS INFORMATION ON TO DIRECTOR DUMONT ONCE KEEFER HAS GONE TO DRUID HILLS.
NOW, IF YOU'LL EXCUSE ME, I HAVE A LIFE TO GET BACK TO.

DRINKING ALONE AND WATCHING *GILMORE GIRLS* RERUNS? SOME LIFE.

WHAT DO YOU WANT FROM ME?
CALL THE DIRECTOR NOW. GET THIS DEAL CALLED OFF AND WE'LL SET A TRAP FOR KEEFER.
NO. I HAVE MY ORDERS.

C'MON, BUDDY. TAKE THAT STICK OUT OF YOUR ASS AND DO THE RIGHT THING HERE.

FINE, I'LL CALL.
BUT DON'T *EVER* CALL ME "BUDDY."

I DON'T KNOW WHAT YOU THINK I CAN DO TO HELP, BUT YOU'VE REACHED THE END OF THE LINE HERE.

HERE. MY *NOTES.* WE'LL GO OVER THEM TOGETHER.
CHARLES... THIS WON'T *SOLVE* THE PROBLEM...

YOU THINK THE PROBLEM IS THAT I'VE GONE *CRAZY.* BUT I *HAVEN'T.*
THE PROBLEM IS THAT I CAN'T TURN IT *OFF.*

AND IF *ANYTHING* IS MAKING ME CRAZY, IT'S THE NOTION OF NOT BEING ABLE TO BE *SEEN* OR *RECOGNIZED* FOR MY WORK.

I'VE ACHIEVED THIS GREAT THING, BUT I CAN'T GET THE CREDIT BECAUSE I'M *NOT* THERE.
NO ONE CAN SEE ME.

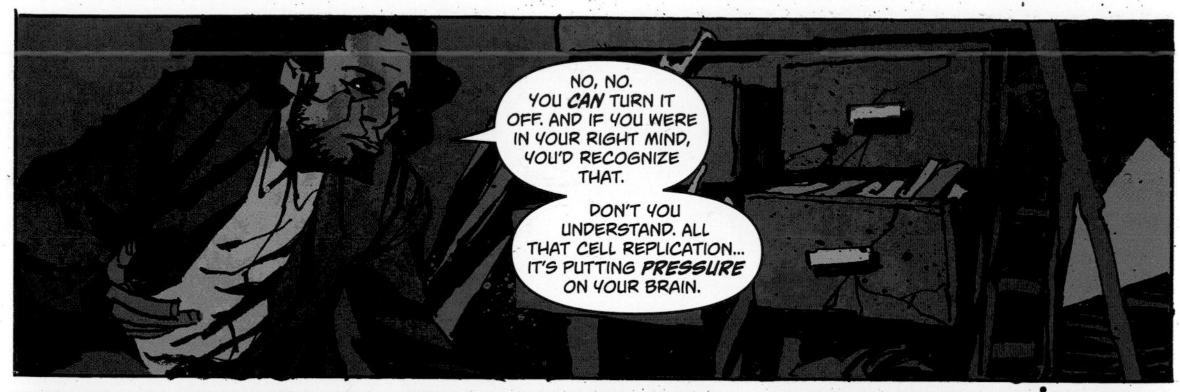
NO, NO. YOU CAN TURN IT OFF. AND IF YOU WERE IN YOUR RIGHT MIND, YOU'D RECOGNIZE THAT.
DON'T YOU UNDERSTAND. ALL THAT CELL REPLICATION... IT'S PUTTING PRESSURE ON YOUR BRAIN.

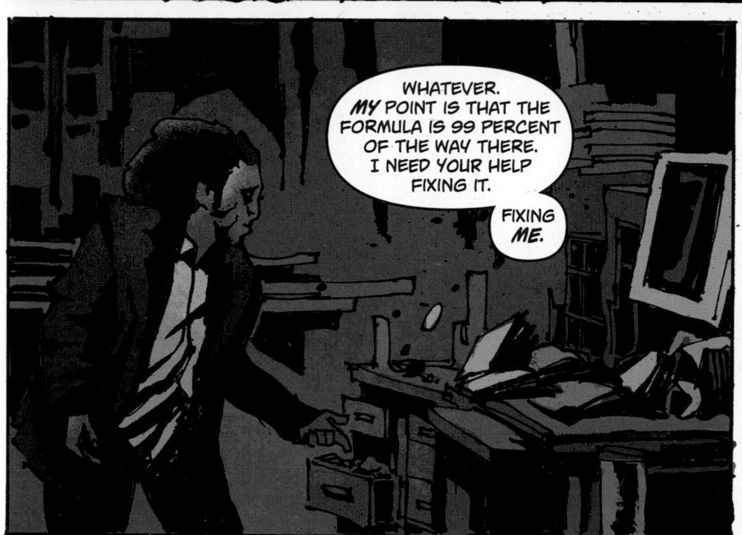
WHATEVER. MY POINT IS THAT THE FORMULA IS 99 PERCENT OF THE WAY THERE. I NEED YOUR HELP FIXING IT.
FIXING ME.

DON'T YOU WANT TO PROVE TO THE WORLD THAT WE CAN DO THIS? DON'T YOU WANT THIS TRIUMPH?

TRUST ME, CHARLES. I KNOW WHAT IT'S LIKE TO HAVE SOMETHING GO WRONG. BUT YOU CAN'T JUST SAY IT DOESN'T MATTER, THAT IT WAS ALL IN THE NAME OF SCIENCE.

I'VE... I'VE BEEN TALKING TO SOMEONE. IT HELPS... WITH THE GUILT.

PLEASE. SHE'S DEAD. SO YOU'RE JUST AS CRAZY AS I AM.

KEEFER?

YOU'RE NOT PROPERLY *MOTIVATED*.

CHARLES... DON'T BE RIDICULOUS...

MAYBE IF THE SITUATION HITS A LITTLE CLOSER TO HOME.

FREEZE!

YOU CAN'T SHOOT WHAT YOU CAN'T **SEE**.
I CAN SEE WHAT YOU'RE HOLDING.

HE FELT TRAPPED. HE'D BEEN DRIVEN INSANE BY HIS OWN WORK. YOU SHOULDN'T HAVE KILLED HIM.

HE WAS PLANNING TO INJECT YOU WITH SOMETHING THAT WOULD HAVE KILLED YOU OR DRIVEN YOU CRAZY. SO... YOU'RE WELCOME.

YOU KNOW, A LOT OF PEOPLE THINK I'M ALREADY CRAZY. WOULD YOU SHOOT ME?

I NEED TO GET BACK TO THE STATION. LET'S GO.

BRAZIL. TWO WEEKS LATER.
‹WE'VE RUN OUT OF PLACES TO PUT THE SICK, SIR.›

‹I'VE NEVER SEEN ANYTHING LIKE IT. THEY CAN'T KEEP ANYTHING DOWN. NO FOOD, NO WATER... IF THIS KEEPS UP, IT'S JUST A MATTER OF TIME...›

‹SSH... REST...›

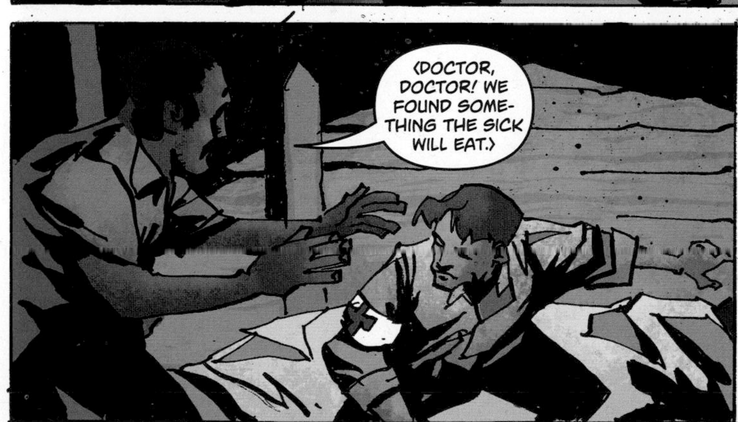
‹DOCTOR, DOCTOR! WE FOUND SOME-THING THE SICK WILL EAT.›

BLAM!!
<...US!>

BAD MEDICINE

KILLING MOON

PORTLAND, MAINE
NO! STOP! PLEASE, NO!

HELP ME! SOMEONE... HELP!

HELP!
SOMEONE... PLEASE...

HUFF HUFF
STOP! STOP!

WHAT'S THE MATTER, MISS?
HE... HE'S CHASING ME. HE... WON'T... STOP...

HOLY SHIT!

BLAM!
BLAM!
GRRR
STAY BACK!

OHMYGOD, OHMYGOD, OHMYGOD...

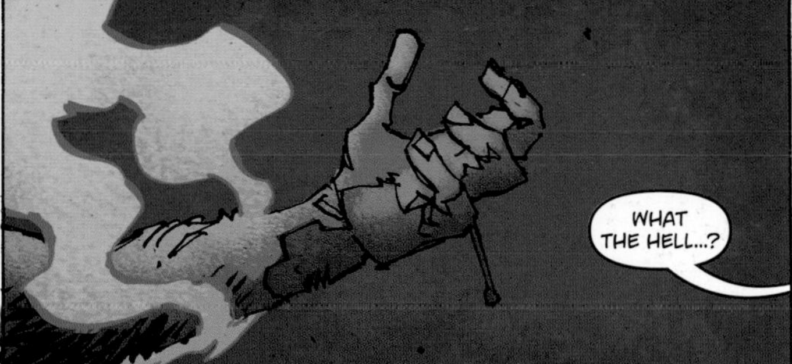
WHAT THE HELL...?

WE'RE LOOKING AT THE VIDEO FROM THE POLICE CAR'S DASHBOARD CAMERA.

CLICK
AND THIS WAS LAST NIGHT?

OFFICES OF THE C.D.C., DRUID HILLS, GEORGIA.
10:47 P.M. TO BE EXACT. WE HAD THE VIDEO MESSENGERED TO US ALONG WITH THE M.E.'S PRELIMINARY FINDINGS.

LABS SHOW TRACES OF AN *INFECTION* IN THE DEAD BOY.
COULD A RETROVIRUS ACCOUNT FOR THIS KIND OF TRANSFORMATION?

NO IDEA. THAT'S WHY I CALLED *YOU* IN.

I'D LIKE YOU TO LEAD AN INVESTIGATIVE TEAM. HEAD UP TO PORTLAND WHERE THE INCIDENT TOOK PLACE.
NO I.D. ON THE BOY YET, BUT A CLASS RING FOR DEER FALLS HIGH SCHOOL WAS FOUND ON HIM. IT'S A SMALL TOWN JUST OUTSIDE PORTLAND.

DIRECTOR DUMONT... WHILE I APPRECIATE THE FACT YOU WERE WILLING TO RESCIND THE OFFER TO DR. KEEFER UPON LEARNING OF HIS CONDITION, I DON'T KNOW HOW KEEN I AM ON WORKING FOR THE GOVERNMENT.

DR. HORNE... THERE ARE SO MANY THINGS SCIENCE CAN'T YET EXPLAIN. ISN'T THAT WHAT YOU'VE BEEN TELLING WHOEVER WILL LISTEN?
THIS IS WHY WE WENT ON OUR JOURNEY, RANDAL. TO PREPARE YOU FOR THIS.

FINE. I'M IN.

EXCELLENT. OUR FIRST ORDER OF BUSINESS IS TO DETERMINE THE NATURE OF THE INFECTION AND WHETHER OR NOT IT IS *CONTAGIOUS*.
NOK NOK

DIRECTOR... I REALLY MUST REGISTER MY DISSATISFACTION AT THE NATURE OF THIS NEW ASSIGNMENT. DR. HORNE IS A DISREPUTABLE, UNRELIABLE--

DON'T LISTEN TO HIM! IT'S NOT A FULL DAY UNLESS THE GREAT DR. TEAGUE HAS INSERTED HIS FOOT IN HIS MOUTH AT *LEAST* SIX TIMES.
GREAT TO SEE YOU AGAIN, DOC. I AM SUPER EXCITED. I MEAN, C'MON? WEREWOLVES!

AS DR. HOGARTH HAS SO... ENTHUSIASTICALLY STATED, THERE IS SOME CONCERN THAT THIS INFECTION COULD BE RELATED TO SOME SORT OF LYCANTHROPY.
IF THAT IS THE CASE, THEN TIME IS OF THE ESSENCE. LAST NIGHT WAS THE FIRST NIGHT OF THE FULL MOON. IF MYTHOLOGY HOLDS TRUE, THAT LEAVES TWO MORE NIGHTS OF POTENTIAL WOLF ACTIVITY.

UNDERSTOOD. WE'LL LEAVE IMMEDIATELY.
UH, NOT TO BE ALL WET BLANKET LIKE... BUT IF WE'RE GONNA BE FIGHTING WEREWOLVES, THIS NERD BRIGADE'S GONNA GET THEIR ASSES KICKED.

DEVLIN
BROWER
JOHNSON
BAILEY
NICE WORK ON PUTTING DOWN THE BAILEY MURDER.

72ND POLICE PRECINCT, BROOKLYN, NEW YORK.
SO, WHO DID IT? COUNT DRACULA?
I HEARD BIGFOOT CAME TO TOWN, THOUGHT HE'D SEE THE STATUE OF LIBERTY, COMMIT A MURDER...

MY FOOT ISN'T SO BIG THAT I CAN'T SHOVE IT UP YOUR ASS, FRANKLIN!
HUFFMAN!

MY OFFICE. NOW.

LISTEN, CAPTAIN, FRANKLIN'S BEEN RIDING ME EVER SINCE--
CAN IT, HUFFMAN.
YOU NEED TO STOP TALKING ABOUT THE KEEFER CASE. LOOK, THE GOVERNMENT TOOK ALL THE FILES. WE GOT NO PROOF OF ANY-THING. BEST TO CALL KEEFER CRAZY AND MOVE ON.

BUT CAPTAIN--
NO. WE'RE DONE. TAKE THE REST OF THE DAY OFF.

MERLIN, I'M HOME!

HEY, BUDDY... ANYONE HERE? NO? GOOD, BOY. IT'S GOOD TO SEE YOU, TOO.

You have no new messages.

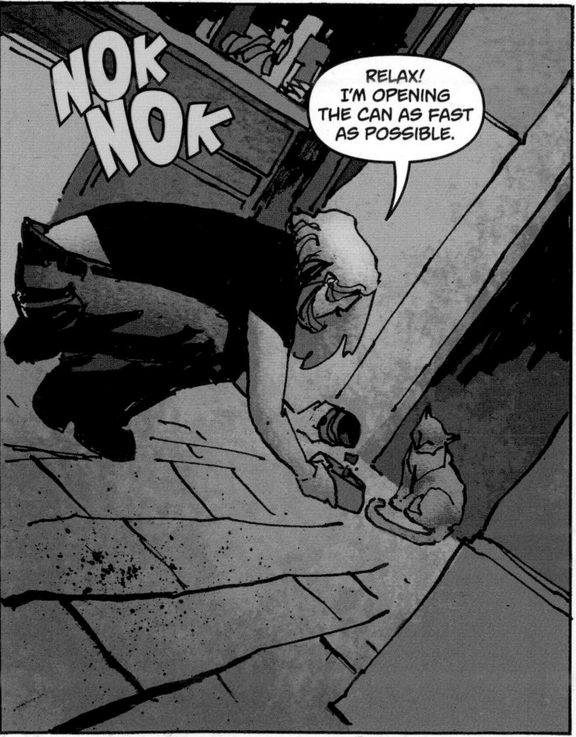
NOK NOK
RELAX! I'M OPENING THE CAN AS FAST AS POSSIBLE.

DETECTIVE HUFFMAN...
OH, YAY.

I KNOW IT'S BEEN A WHILE, BUT THE C.D.C. IS PUTTING TOGETHER A TEAM.

AN UNIDENTIFIED BOY WAS SHOT AND KILLED BY A COP IN MAINE. THEY SAY HE'S GOT AN *INFECTION*.
HEY! DON'T YOU WANT TO EVEN **HEAR** THE OFFER BEFORE YOU SAY NO?

DR. HOGARTH THINKS IT MIGHT BE WEREWOLVES...

I KNOW IT SOUNDS CRAZY, BUT--

LET'S GO.

PORTLAND POLICE DEPARTMENT.
DETECTIVE HUFFMAN? I'M OFFICER WILENSKY. I WAS THE ONE ON THE SCENE.
WHAT'S A COP FROM THE N.Y.P.D. DOING UP HERE INVESTIGATING THIS CASE?
I'M ACTUALLY WORKING WITH THE C.D.C. I WAS HOPING YOU COULD TELL ME IF YOU'VE GOTTEN ANY FURTHER IN I.D.ING THE BOY--
C.D.C., HUH?
LOOK, YOU GOTTA TALK TO THE GOVERNMENT GUYS AND GET MY TAPE BACK.
EXCUSE ME?
THE VIDEO FROM MY CAR...? THEY CONFISCATED IT. SAID IT WAS TOP GOVERNMENT PRIORITY OR SOME OTHER BUREAUCRATIC BULLSHIT.
I'M SORRY, OFFICER WILENSKY, BUT--
YOU DON'T UNDERSTAND. NO ONE BELIEVES ME. THE ONLY REASON I SHOT THAT KID WAS BECAUSE HE WAS SOME KIND OF RABID MONSTER.
BUT THEY ALL THINK I'M CRAZY TALKING ABOUT BOY WOLVES AND THE LIKE.
YOU HAVE NO IDEA WHAT THAT'S LIKE. IF I DON'T GET MY TAPE BACK, I'M RUINED.

DR. HORNE... I'M DR. PENNINGTON. DEPUTY DIRECTOR DUMONT PHONED TO LET US KNOW YOU'D BE COMING. I ASSUME YOU'RE HERE TO SEE THE BODY.
YES, THANK YOU.

IF YOU'RE INTERESTED, THE GIRL HE ATTACKED JUST CAME IN ABOUT 20 MINUTES AGO ASKING TO SEE A DOCTOR. SHE'S WITH ONE OF OUR INTERNS NOW.
VERY INTERESTED.
YOU TWO GO AHEAD. I'LL TALK TO THE GIRL.

I'M NOT SURE IF HE WAS SICK, JENNA. WE DON'T HAVE ALL THE LABS BACK YET.
MAYBE YOU SHOULD TELL ME WHAT HAPPENED.
I... I...

IT'S OKAY. TAKE IT SLOW. YOU CAME IN FOR A REASON.
I JUST WANT TO KNOW IF HE WAS... SICK.

I THINK--
DR. ANDERSON... IF YOU'LL EXCUSE US.

MISS WALSH, THIS IS DR. HORNE FROM THE C.D.C.

C.D.C.? THAT'S, LIKE, FOR REALLY BAD DISEASES, RIGHT?
WE'RE HOPING YOU CAN TELL US WHAT YOU SAW OF YOUR ATTACKER.

I... I WAS WALKING HOME. IT WAS DARK. HE WAS A GUY... WOLF... CREATURE.

A GUY, OR A WOLF? OR DID YOU SEE HIM TRANSFORM? CAN YOU DESCRIBE THE PROCESS?
I... YES... NO...

NO. LEAVE ME ALONE. I JUST WANT TO GO HOME.
WAIT. I NEED TO ASK YOU A FEW MORE QUESTIONS.
ENOUGH!

MY DAUGHTER IS A MESS, DOCTOR. SHE HASN'T EATEN OR SLEPT SINCE LAST NIGHT. I DON'T THINK THIS TYPE OF BADGERING IS APPROPRIATE. WE'LL BE GOING NOW.

MRS. WALSH, WAIT.
I SEE YOUR BEDSIDE MANNER HASN'T IMPROVED ONE BIT.

I THINK YOU MAY NEED A DOCTOR WHO IS A LITTLE BETTER AT DEALING WITH PEOPLE.

QUEENS, NEW YORK.
ARE YOU OUT OF YOUR MIND? I HAVE A JOB! I LIKE MY JOB.

I'M TALKING ABOUT THE OPPORTUNITY OF A LIFETIME. YOU WOULDN'T BELIEVE THE THINGS I'VE SEEN.
RIGHT NOW WE'RE LOOKING INTO A POSSIBLE DISEASE THAT CAN TURN A HUMAN BEING INTO A WEREWOLF.

WEREWOLVES? ARE YOU INSANE? I MEAN, MORE THAN USUAL?
THE THINGS WE'RE DOING, JAMES... IT'S INCREDIBLE.

MAYBE. BUT IT'S NOT WHAT I'M INTERESTED IN.
EXACTLY. YOU CARE ABOUT THE PEOPLE. THAT'S WHY I NEED YOU.

I WAS NEVER GOOD WITH PEOPLE, JAMES. SCIENCE? YES. BUT MEDICINE? THE PART THAT DEALS WITH THE PATIENTS...?
THAT'S WHERE YOU'RE A GENIUS. I'VE GOT A TERRIFIED GIRL UP IN MAINE WHO MAY BE THE KEY TO HELPING US.

PLEASE. I NEED YOUR HELP.

LET ME REITERATE... THIS IS NOT A PERMANENT THING. I'LL HELP THIS TIME AND THIS TIME ONLY.

SURE THING...

HELLO?
HI MRS. WALSH, I'M DR. JAMES LUCAS. WE WERE HOPING WE COULD TALK TO YOUR DAUGHTER.

YOU! HAVEN'T YOU DONE ENOUGH?
JENNA IS MISSING! SHE SNUCK OUT SOMETIME LAST NIGHT AND STILL HASN'T COME HOME!
I'M SORRY?

GO AWAY AND LEAVE US ALONE!

WOW. YOUR PEOPLE SKILLS REALLY HAVEN'T IMPROVED.
I *TOLD* YOU I NEEDED YOUR HELP.

JUST SO EVERYONE KNOWS, I WON'T BE PART OF A GOVERNMENT COVER-UP.

UM... NOTED?

I'M SERIOUS. OFFICER WILENSKY SHOT A KID, AND THE ONLY EVIDENCE THAT IT WAS A RIGHTEOUS SHOOTING IS NOW IN OUR POSSESSION.

HE PROMISED TO LOOK INTO JENNA'S WHEREABOUTS AND CALL ME AS SOON AS HE KNOWS ANYTHING. AND IN RETURN, I ***WILL*** MAKE SURE HE GETS THAT TAPE BACK.

ARE WE ALL ***CLEAR*** ON THAT?

YOU HAVE MY WORD, DETECTIVE.

I HIGHLY DOUBT IT WILL BE YOUR CALL, DR. HORNE.

THEN I WILL ***MAKE*** IT MY CALL.

WHAT'S THAT SMELL...? OH... RIGHT. CLEAN AIR.

GREETINGS. WELCOME TO DEER FALLS. FROM THE LOOKS OF THAT VEHICLE YOU'RE THE C.D.C. PEOPLE WE WERE TOLD ABOUT.
DR. RANDAL HORNE.

WE'RE TRYING TO I.D. A BOY WHO WAS KILLED IN PORTLAND TWO NIGHTS AGO. HE HAD A DEER FALLS SENIOR CLASS RING ON HIS HAND, SO WE THOUGHT WE'D SEE IF ANYONE HERE KNEW WHO HE WAS.

NOPE. CAN'T SAY AS I RECOGNIZE HIM.
BUT HONESTLY, DR. HORNE, I TOLD THE SAME THING TO THE PORTLAND POLICE WHEN THEY SENT SOMEONE OUT HERE YESTERDAY.

YOU DON'T MIND IF WE LOOK AROUND, DO YOU? SHOW HIS PICTURE TO SOME OF THE TOWNSPEOPLE?
YOU GO RIGHT AHEAD. BUT WE'RE A PRETTY SMALL COMMUNITY HERE. IF I DON'T KNOW HIM, I DOUBT ANYONE ELSE WILL.

DEFINITELY NOT ONE OF MY PATIENTS.
MAYBE A FORMER PATIENT? SOMEONE WHO USED TO LIVE IN TOWN...?
NOBODY EVER MOVES OUT OF DEER FALLS. IT'S A WONDERFUL PLACE. NO ONE LEAVES.

AND THIS IS THE WHOLE SENIOR CLASS? WHY HAVE YOUR OWN SCHOOL THEN? COULDN'T YOU KIDS JUST GO TO THE REGIONAL HIGH SCHOOL?
BECAUSE WE'RE DEER FALLS KIDS. OF COURSE WE GO TO SCHOOL HERE.

WHAT? IS THERE A LAW?
RANDAL...

WELL... I...
NO. WE'VE NEVER SEEN HIM BEFORE.

I SEE YOU LEFT. RECEIVED YOUR DEGREE AT THE UNIVERSITY OF PORTLAND.
AH, YES. BUT I'M RARE. AND I CAME BACK. VERY FEW PEOPLE EVER LEAVE THE TOWN.

NO. NEVER.
ABSOLUTELY.
ARE YOU SURE?

AS YOU SUSPECTED, WE FOUND NO ONE WHO COULD I.D. THE BOY.
SORRY YOU WASTED YOUR TIME.
HOWEVER, I *DID* NOTICE... PEOPLE IN THIS--

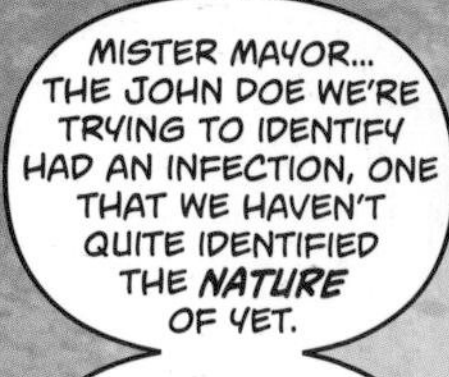

MISTER MAYOR... THE JOHN DOE WE'RE TRYING TO IDENTIFY HAD AN INFECTION, ONE THAT WE HAVEN'T QUITE IDENTIFIED THE *NATURE* OF YET.
AND WE HAVE REASON TO BELIEVE THAT EVEN IF HE WASN'T FROM DEER FALLS, HE MIGHT HAVE PASSED THROUGH HERE AT SOME POINT.
WE'D LIKE YOUR PERMISSION TO COLLECT BLOOD SAMPLES FROM THE LOCALS TO MAKE SURE IT WASN'T SOMETHING HE CONTRACTED WHILE HERE OR SOMETHING HE SPREAD.

ABSOLUTELY NOT! OUT OF THE QUESTION!
MAYOR DURNING, PLEASE... ANY INFORMATION WE CAN GATHER...
I SAID--
BILL...

ALLOW ME TO INTRODUCE MYSELF. I'M SHERIFF POWELL.
AND IF YOU'RE SAYING OUR LITTLE TOWN COULD BE IN DANGER, THEN OF COURSE WE WILL DO WHATEVER WE CAN TO HELP. ISN'T THAT RIGHT, MAYOR?

OF COURSE, SHERIFF.

BUT OF COURSE. I WOULD NEVER ASK THE TOWNSPEOPLE TO DO SOMETHING I WASN'T WILLING TO DO MYSELF.
HEADED OVER RIGHT NOW. CARE TO ACCOMPANY ME?
YOU GO ON AHEAD. I'VE STILL GOT MY CAT TO FEED.

BURNING THE MIDNIGHT OIL?

YOU MAY HAVE A SMALL TOWN, BUT WE'RE STILL ONLY ABOUT HALFWAY THROUGH THE SAMPLES.

THOUGH YOU'LL BE HAPPY TO KNOW THAT THUS FAR, EVERYONE'S TESTING NEGATIVE.

ANYTHING I CAN DO TO HELP?

YOU CAN *GO*.

OF COURSE. GOOD NIGHT.

WHAT?

CLK
CLK
CLK

GRRRWLL

PORTLAND, MAINE.
DR. PENNINGTON...?

SIR...? I'M TRYING TO FINISH UP SOME PAPERWORK AND I WAS JUST WONDERING...
I CAN'T FIND ANY OF THE TEST RESULTS FOR JENNA WALSH.

WHO?

THE GIRL WHO CAME IN YESTERDAY AFTER BEING ATTACKED BY THE JOHN DOE?
RIGHT. YES. THERE WERE *NO* TESTS DONE.
WHAT?
THERE WAS NO *NEED*. THE DEAD BOY NEVER ACTUALLY ATTACKED HER.

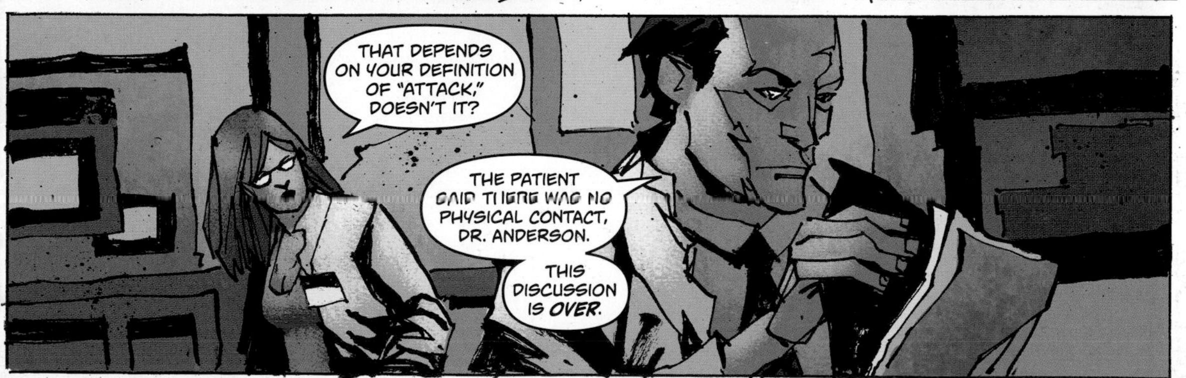
THAT DEPENDS ON YOUR DEFINITION OF "ATTACK," DOESN'T IT?
THE PATIENT SAID THERE WAS NO PHYSICAL CONTACT, DR. ANDERSON.
THIS DISCUSSION IS *OVER*.

DEER FALLS, MAINE.
THAT WAS DR. PENNINGTON FROM PORTLAND CITY HOSPITAL.
MAN, THAT GUY IS A PIECE OF WORK...

ARROGANT DOCTOR, GO FIGURE.

IT WAS A STANDARD C.Y.A. CALL. WANTED US TO UNDER-STAND THAT THERE WAS NO BLOOD WORK ON JENNA WALSH. AND EXPLAIN WHY.
SO WE'VE GOT NO WAY OF KNOWING IF SHE WAS INFECTED?

PENNINGTON SWEARS UP AND DOWN THAT THERE WAS NO ***CONTACT***.

WHY DON'T I FEEL REASSURED?
BECAUSE YOU'RE A ***COP***. TRUST ME, I DON'T LIKE IT EITHER THAT WE NEVER GOT TO REALLY TALK TO HER.
WHEN WE'RE DONE HERE, I'D LIKE ANOTHER CHANCE TO--

GRRRR...

CAN I HELP YOU?
MRS. WALSH, I'M DR. ANDERSON. I EXAMINED YOUR DAUGHTER YESTERDAY AT THE HOSPITAL. I WAS HOPING I COULD TALK TO HER FOR A FEW MINUTES.

SHE'S... SHE'S NOT HERE. IS SOME-THING WRONG?
I JUST WANTED TO FOLLOW-UP WITH HER. SHE WAS UNDERSTANDABLY VERY UPSET. DO YOU KNOW WHEN SHE'LL BE BACK?

JENNA WALSH HAS BEEN MISSING SINCE LAST NIGHT. YOU SAID YOU WERE HER DOCTOR?
YES... I'M SORRY, MISSING? WHAT HAPPENED?
I... I DON'T KNOW... SHE SNUCK OUT AND HASN'T... COME HOME...

I'M SO SORRY. LISTEN, MRS. WALSH, HAS JENNA BEEN SEEING ANYONE? A BOY-FRIEND, MAYBE?
NO. NOT THAT I KNOW OF. WHY DO YOU ASK? DO YOU THINK SHE RAN OFF WITH SOMEONE?

NO, IT'S NOT THAT. BUT SHE WAS SO CONCERNED ABOUT THE WELL-BEING OF THE BOY WHO ATTACKED HER. IT SEEMED MORE LIKE CONCERN FOR A FRIEND OR BOYFRIEND.
CERTAINLY NOT A ***STRANGER***.

THERE ***HAVE*** BEEN A BUNCH OF HUSHED PHONE CALLS RECENTLY. BUT YOU KNOW HOW TEEN-AGERS ARE.
MRS. WALSH, DO I HAVE YOUR PERMISSION TO SEARCH JENNA'S BEDROOM?

I DON'T KNOW MANY DOCTORS WHO MAKE HOUSE CALLS. WHY ARE YOU SO INTERESTED IN JENNA?
THE C.D.C. SENT A TEAM TO INVESTIGATE THE JOHN DOE WHO ATTACKED MY PATIENT. AND JENNA WAS EXTREMELY *AGITATED* WHEN SHE CAME TO THE E.R.

I DON'T *BLAME* HER. I *SAW* THE THING THAT WAS CHASING HER. THAT WOULD FREAK ME THE FUCK OUT TOO.
OH, EXCUSE MY LANGUAGE.

I CAN'T SHAKE THE FEELING THAT SHE MUST HAVE *KNOWN* HIM. AND IF SHE DID, THEN MAYBE SHE KNEW HIS FRIENDS OR HIS FAMILY.

WELL, CHECK THIS OUT... YOU'D MAKE QUITE THE DETECTIVE, DOCTOR.
DAMN. NO WALLET, THOUGH. STILL NO I.D.

I KNOW WHERE TO LOOK FOR JENNA.

RANDAL!

BLAM!

SPK!

GRRR

SSSSSSS

WHAT... WHY DID HE JUST RUN OFF LIKE THAT?

SILVER BULLETS.

THAT ACTUALLY WORKS?
I GUESS SO. WASN'T SURE, ACTUALLY. BUT SINCE YOU MENTIONED ***WEREWOLVES***, I TRACKED SOME DOWN IN PORTLAND.

DIDN'T ***KILL*** HIM THOUGH. HURT LIKE ***HELL***, I THINK. AND SLOWED HIM DOWN ENOUGH THAT HE RETREATED.
SHIT! HUFFMAN...

THIS ISN'T FUNNY. YOU CALL US OVER, AND THEN LOCK US OUT?
I CAN'T LET YOU IN. I'VE BEEN COMPROMISED.
WAIT... YOU RAN INTO SOMEONE INFECTED?
CHASED IT OFF, BUT DR. LUCAS IS DEAD, AND MY ARM'S BEEN SCRATCHED.
NOT GOOD.
IF FOLKLORE IS TO BE BELIEVED, THIS THING WILL BE OUT UNTIL THE MOON GOES DOWN. THIS WHOLE TOWN IS IN DANGER.
GO DOOR TO DOOR. GET THEM TO LOCK THEMSELVES IN. AND TAKE DOCTOR HORNE--
I'M STAYING HERE.

HAVE YOU SEEN EITHER OF THESE TWO KIDS?

THE BOY, TWO NIGHTS AGO. THE GIRL, SAME NIGHT. AND MAYBE TONIGHT?
HEY, SHE SHOWED ME I.D. LOOKED TOTALLY LEGIT.

WE'RE NOT HERE ABOUT FAKE I.D.S. SHE HASN'T BEEN HOME IN 24 HOURS. HER MOTHER IS WORRIED.
YEAH, SHE CAME IN A LITTLE WHILE AGO. LOOKED KINDA FREAKED OUT ACTUALLY.

HOW'D YOU RECOGNIZE THE STAMP ON HER HAND? I WOULDN'T THINK DOCTORS WOULD GET A LOT OF TIME OFF FOR BAR-HOPPING.
WAY TOO MANY FRIDAY NIGHT SHIFTS AT THE E.R.

THERE!

JENNA! WAIT!

WE DON'T KNOW ANY-THING RIGHT NOW. SHE'LL PROBABLY TURN AND THEN EAT HIM AS A MID-NIGHT SNACK.
UH, HELLO...? IS THERE ANY COMPASSION LURKING WITHIN YOU?
OF COURSE I FEEL BAD. BUT THERE'S NOTHING WE CAN DO. RANDAL HORNE WOULD BE OF MORE USE OUT HERE SAVING UNINFECTED PEOPLE.
BUT I SUSPECT HE'S BEEN A HEAD CASE SINCE THE DAY HE KILLED HIS PATIENT.
OH MAN, OH MAN, OH MAN. DO YOU THINK SHE'LL BE OKAY? IS THERE ANY-THING DR. HORNE CAN DO FOR HER?
HE'S AN IDIOT.
I TOLD THE DEPUTY DIRECTOR THAT SHE SHOULD HAVE PUT ME IN CHARGE.
NOK NOK
I'M JUST GOING TO PRETEND WE DIDN'T HAVE THIS CONVERSATION, OKAY?
HELLO...?

DID WE CATCH YOU AT A BAD TIME, MR. MAYOR?
NO, NO... I WAS JUST... ASLEEP.

ASLEEP? AT 9:30 AT NIGHT? I MEAN, I KNOW DEER FALLS ISN'T EXACTLY PARTY CENTRAL, BUT STILL...
IS THERE SOMETHING I CAN DO FOR YOU GENTLEMEN?

THERE WAS A WEREWOLF ATTACK TONIGHT, MR. MAYOR. ONE OF OUR MEN WAS KILLED.
KILLED?
WE NEED TO PUT THE TOWN ON LOCKDOWN. EVERYONE IN THEIR HOUSES. NO ONE OUT FOR ANY REASON. NOT UNTIL SUNRISE.

YES. OF COURSE. JUST LET ME PUT SOME CLOTHES ON.
WAIT HERE. I'LL BE RIGHT BACK.

WELL?
WELL WHAT?

SOMETHING DOESN'T SMELL RIGHT. I'M GONNA LOOK AROUND.
CARE TO JOIN?

SO...?
ANYTHING?

WHAT THE FUCK? HAVE YOU DONE ANYTHING?

HOLY SHIT...

YOU LOCKED YOURSELF IN HERE TO DIE.

JENNA! I JUST WANT TO TALK TO YOU.
WAIT HERE. I'LL GET HER.
I DON'T KNOW...
PLEASE. NO OFFENSE, YOU'RE A NICE GUY. BUT YOU'RE A COP. AND JENNA'S SPOOKED.
JENNA, PLEASE... IT'S DR. ANDERSON. I'M ALONE.
PLEASE DON'T RUN AWAY. I JUST WANT TO HELP.
YOU CAME TO SEE ME YESTERDAY. REMEMBER? YOU HAD QUESTIONS. LET ME HELP.
CAN YOU TELL ME ABOUT THE BOY? THE ONE WHO ATTACKED YOU... YOU KNEW HIM, YES? IS THIS WHERE YOU MET HIM? DID YOU KNOW HIS NAME?
HIS NAME WAS SCOTT.

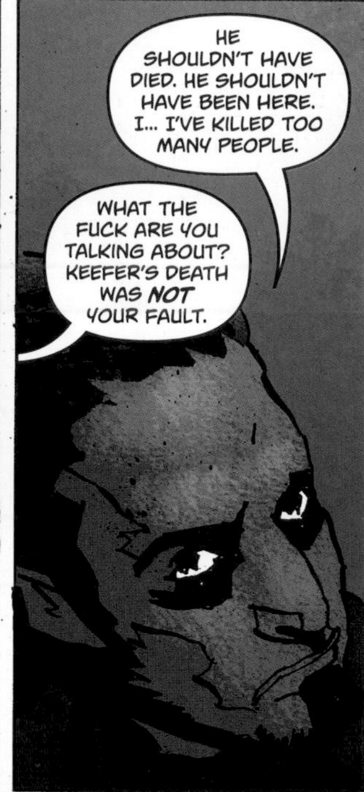

"THERE WAS A DRUG. TESOVAC. IT WAS SUPPOSED TO BLOCK THE ENDOTHELIN RECEPTORS AND PREVENT ACUTE HEART FAILURE.

"I WAS VERY COZY WITH THE PHARMACEUTICAL COMPANY THAT WAS TESTING IT, AND I PUSHED REBECCA TO LET US TREAT HER WITH IT.

"JAMES DISAGREED."

HE WAS UNCONVINCED BY THE COMPANY REPS, AND HE WAS RIGHT.
NOT ONLY DID TESOVAC FAIL TO PREVENT ACUTE HEART FAILURE, IT CAUSED UNCONTROLLABLE BLEEDING DURING SURGERY.
I KILLED HER. MY ARROGANCE KILLED HER. I CARRY HER WITH ME ALWAYS.
AND NOW... JAMES DIDN'T WANT TO COME BUT I BEGGED HIM.
I KILLED THE MOST DECENT MAN I KNOW.

OKAY. SO YOU **KNEW** HIM? HOW DID YOU TWO MEET?
HERE. AT THIS CLUB. I WAS WITH A FRIEND. HER SISTER IS IN COLLEGE AND HAD GOTTEN US FAKE I.D.S. WE THOUGHT IT'D BE A KICK TO SEE IF WE COULD GET SOME GUYS TO NOTICE US.

IT'S OKAY. GO ON.
SCOTT AND I JUST KINDA HIT IT OFF. I GAVE HIM MY CELL NUMBER AND HE STARTED CALLING. SO WE'D TALK AND STUFF. FOR HOURS.
DID HE GIVE YOU HIS LAST NAME?
NO. AND I DIDN'T ASK. I KNOW. IT WAS **STUPID**.

MY PARENTS WERE GONNA BE OUT THE OTHER NIGHT. SO I MET HIM HERE, AND THEN I... INVITED HIM BACK TO MY HOUSE.

I KNOW THIS IS HARD, JENNA. BUT I **NEED** YOU TO TELL ME EVERYTHING.

GROW THE FUCK UP, DOC.
I MEAN FOR GOD'S SAKE... CRY ME A FUCKING A RIVER! WE *ALL* HAVE OUR SECRET PAIN.
I'M SORRY YOU'VE GOT THESE DEAD BODIES ON YOUR CONSCIENCE, BUT YOU'RE ABOUT TO HAVE ONE *MORE!*
I AM GOING TO TURN INTO A GODDAMN *WEREWOLF* IF YOU DON'T FIND ME A *CURE!*
I'M GOING TO NEED TEAGUE.

SO, DR. HIGH AND MIGHTY NEEDS ME NOW?
HA. POT, KETTLE.

HE'S A CARDIOLOGIST, TEAGUE. YOU'RE THE PATHOLOGIST. DON'T BE AN ASS.
YOUR POWERS OF PERSUASION ARE STAGGERING, DETECTIVE.

UM... I THINK WE MAY HAVE SOME TROUBLE.

OH YEAH? CHECK THIS OUT.

WE DEFINITELY HAVE TROUBLE.

MY FRIEND SAID I WAS CRAZY. HAVING A GUY I BARELY KNEW OVER. BUT HE WAS REALLY SWEET.
THEN... WE, UH, WELL... WE STARTED MAKING OUT.
AND...? DID IT PROGRESS PAST THAT?
HE... HE HAD HIS HAND UP UNDER MY SHIRT. AND... YOU KNOW...
I DON'T MEAN TO BE TOO PERSONAL, JENNA. BUT... DID YOU SLEEP WITH HIM?
YES.
DR. ANDERSON...? I... I DON'T FEEL SO GOOD.

JENNA...?
WHAT IS IT?

MAUNA KEA, HAWAII.

FIVE YEARS AGO...

TELL ME WHAT YOU KNOW ABOUT MORPHIC FIELDS, DR. HORNE.

THERE'S A THEORY THAT SAYS ALL LIVING BEINGS ARE CONNECTED BY MORPHIC BONDS INTO GROUPS.

WELL, YES. BUT IS THAT WHAT YOU KNOW? OR SIMPLY WHAT YOU'VE HEARD AND DON'T BELIEVE?

DEFINITELY THE LATTER.

WELL, YOU'RE NOT THE ONLY ONE.

MY DAUGHTER DIED LAST YEAR.

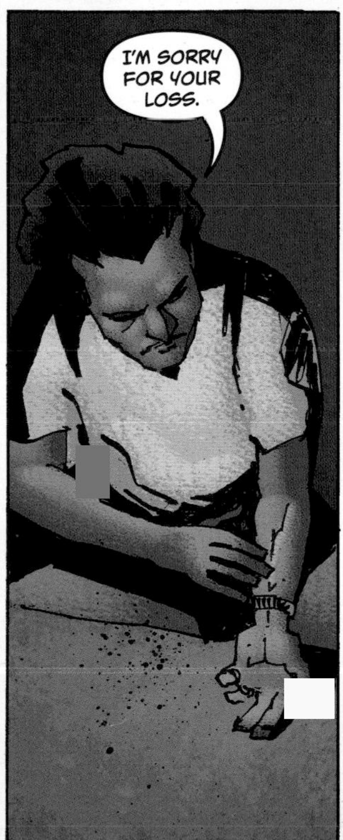

DEER FALLS, MAINE.
TODAY.
HOW VERY ASTUTE OF YOU, DR. HOGARTH.
YOU SAID YOU DIDN'T KNOW HIM...
YES, I KNOW. I *LIED*.
SCOTT IS... WAS MY SON.
DID YOU *KNOW?* DID YOU KNOW HE WAS SOME KIND OF *WOLF* CREATURE?
DR. HOGARTH, I FEEL WE SHOULD BE CONCERNED WITH THE SITUATION OUTSIDE.
ALSO AN ASTUTE OBSERVATION, DR. TEAGUE. BUT A FUTILE ONE, I'M AFRAID.
FOR YOU'LL NEVER GET OUT OF THIS TOWN *ALIVE*.

RUN!
CRAP! CRAP! CRAP!
THIS WAY!
AWOOOOOOO!
AWOOOOOOOO!

J-JENNA...?

GRRR...

OFFICER!
DR. ANDERSON? WHAT HAPP--?

OH HELL!

GRRRRRR
FREEZE!

BRILLIANT. JUST FUCKING BRILLIANT!
DUDE, I KNOW WE'RE SCREWED WHEN YOU START SWEARING.
NOW IS NOT THE TIME FOR YOUR PARTICULAR BRAND OF "HUMOR."
AREN'T YOU ALWAYS SAYING HOW YOU SHOULD'VE BEEN PUT IN CHARGE?
NOW WOULD BE AN EXCELLENT TIME FOR YOU TO DISPLAY SOME OF YOUR BANG-UP LEADERSHIP SKILLS.
BACK OFF!
I MEAN IT! BACK AWAY. I HAVE SILVER BULLETS IN HERE AND I WILL USE THEM.

RUN. NOW.

STAY.
GOOD DOG.

NICE TIMING, DETECTIVE. GOOD THING I'M ONE OF THOSE MODERN MEN WHO HAS NO PROBLEM AT ALL BEING SAVED BY A GOOD LOOKING WOMAN.
DETECTIVE...?

HORNE'S IN THE BACK. HE NEEDS YOU.

WEREWOLF'S BACK. AND APPARENTLY THE TOWNSPEOPLE ARE VERY PROTECTIVE OF IT.

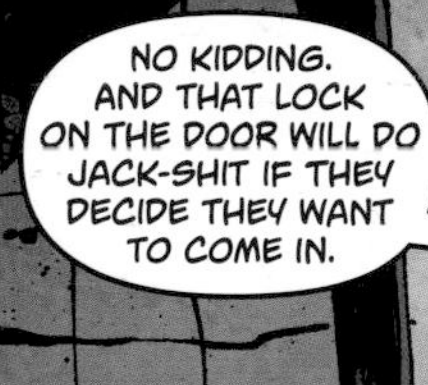
NO KIDDING. AND THAT LOCK ON THE DOOR WILL DO JACK-SHIT IF THEY DECIDE THEY WANT TO COME IN.

ARE YOU OKAY, DETECTIVE? YOUR ARM...

JUST HELP RANDAL WITH A CURE, OKAY?

WHAT DO WE KNOW?
DETECTIVE HUFFMAN SHOT THE WEREWOLF WITH A SILVER BULLET AND GAVE HIM MORE THAN A STANDARD GUNSHOT WOUND.
JUST NOW, OUTSIDE, THEY WERE DEFINITELY WORRIED WHEN I THREATENED TO DO THE SAME THING AGAIN.
NO SHIT! YOU WERE SERIOUS OUT THERE ABOUT SILVER BULLETS?
REALLY, DOCTOR...? WE'RE RESORTING TO FAIRYTALES TO SOLVE THIS?
I CHECKED THIS ENTIRE OFFICE. MOST BANDAGES ARE TREATED WITH TRACE AMOUNTS OF SILVER. NOT HERE.
EVEN THE FRIDGE DOESN'T HAVE A SILVER ANTIBACTERIAL COATING.
IT'S LIKE THIS BUILDING WAS DESIGNED TO BE FREE OF SILVER. IN ANY AMOUNT.
I THINK, JUST MAYBE, THAT THIS FOLKLORE IS REAL.

WHAT THE HELL?
WHY'S SHE LOOK LIKE THAT? WHY'S SHE ONLY PARTIALLY WOLFLIKE?
I DON'T KNOW. MAYBE...

GRRR...

BACK! STAY BACK OR I'LL SHOOT!
GRRRR...

NO! WAIT!
I DON'T THINK THE INFECTION IS AS FAR ALONG YET.

LET ME TALK TO HER.

GREAT. TAKE MY BULLETS. IT'S NOT LIKE I'M GOING TO NEED TO, I DON'T KNOW, SHOOT ANYTHING.
THERE. DONE.
I KNOW IT'S NOT IDEAL, DETECTIVE. BUT SILVER CLEARLY ATTACKS THE INFECTED CELLS AND IT'S NON-TOXIC. MAYBE DR. TEAGUE AND I CAN CONCOCT SOME KIND OF ANTIDOTE WITH THIS.
WHATEVER IT IS, YOU TWO NEED TO WORK FAST.
IT'S LIKE THEY'RE ORGANIZING A LYNCHING OUT THERE.

DO WE THINK THE WHOLE TOWN IS INFECTED? THE WOLF DID ATTACK TO STOP THE BLOOD TESTING.
IT'S UNLIKELY. WE'D GOTTEN THROUGH A HUGE PERCENTAGE OF THE TOWN WITH NO TRACE OF THE RETROVIRUS.
WE MAY EVEN BE LOOKING AT A SINGLE WOLF.
THE MAYOR? TEAGUE AND I FOUND OUT THAT KID IN PORTLAND WAS HIS SON.
AND HE WAS OPPOSED TO THE BLOOD TESTS FROM THE START. BUT WHY ARE THEY SO PROTECTIVE OF HIM?
MORPHIC FIELDS...
DON'T YOU DARE SAY "I TOLD YOU SO."
MORPHIC WHAT NOW?
RUPERT SHELDRAKE PROPOSED THAT THERE WERE FIELDS WITHIN AND AROUND "MORPHIC UNITS" THAT COULD ORGANIZE AND CONTROL A GROUP.
DUDE, LIKE THE FORCE?
MORPHIC FIELDS ARE PART OF WHY ANIMALS ORGANIZE THEMSELVES INSTINCTIVELY IN PACKS. THEY RESPOND TO THE ALPHA. AND HUMANS ARE BOUND BY MORPHIC FIELDS, EVEN IF THEY DON'T KNOW IT.
AN ANIMAL'S KNOWLEDGE OF MORPHIC RESONANCE COMBINED WITH A HUMAN'S CAPACITY FOR MANIPULATION...
...HE COULD USE THE FIELD TO MAKE THE WHOLE TOWN, EVEN IF HUMAN, INTO HIS PACK.

GRRR...
SSH, JENNA... IT'S OKAY...

PUT THE GUN DOWN. PLEASE.
ARE YOU SURE ABOUT THIS, DOCTOR? BECAUSE I'M ***NOT***.

ANIMAL INSTINCT IS A BASIC FIGHT OR FLIGHT. SHE DOESN'T FEEL ***SAFE***.

BUT I'M NOT GOING TO HURT YOU, JENNA. YOU KNOW THAT, ***RIGHT?***
I JUST WANT TO ***HELP*** YOU. LET ME HELP.

DR. ANDERSON...
HELP... ME...

BAM! BAM! BAM!
GUYS, THE NATIVES ARE GETTING RESTLESS.
DETECTIVE HUFFMAN... THERE'S A CHANCE WE'RE NOT GOING TO FINISH THIS--
--IN TIME.
SHIT!
FINISH THE VACCINE, TEAGUE!
WHAT? WHERE ARE YOU GOING?
THOSE TWO ARE SO BUTCH AND SUNDANCE.
BUT YOU AND ME, BUDDY? WE'RE JUST ARTOO AND THREEPIO.

DETECTIVE...
SSH.

I *KEPT* A SILVER BULLET.
JUST ONE?

IF YOU CAN TAKE THE WOLF DOWN, HIS HOLD ON THEM WILL *FADE*. THE FIELD WILL BE BROKEN.
GUESS I BETTER MAKE THIS SHOT *COUNT* THEN.

BAM! BAM!
READY?

KSSSH
BACK AWAY! NOW!

OR YOUR PRECIOUS PACK LEADER GETS A SILVER BULLET STRAIGHT TO THE HEART!

PLEASE, MAYOR DURNING. RELINQUISH THE MORPHIC CONTROL YOU HAVE OVER THESE PEOPLE.

MY MORPHIC WHAT? I HAVE NO IDEA WHAT YOU'RE TALKING ABOUT.

CAREFUL, DOC...
I KNOW WHAT YOU'RE DOING HERE. THIS TOWN, THESE PEOPLE... THEY'RE YOUR *PACK*. THEY WILL LISTEN TO YOU. CALL THEM OFF AND NO ONE HAS TO GET HURT.

YOU CAN'T THREATEN US. WE WILL DO WHAT WE MUST.

BLAM!

AWOOOOOOOOOOOOO!

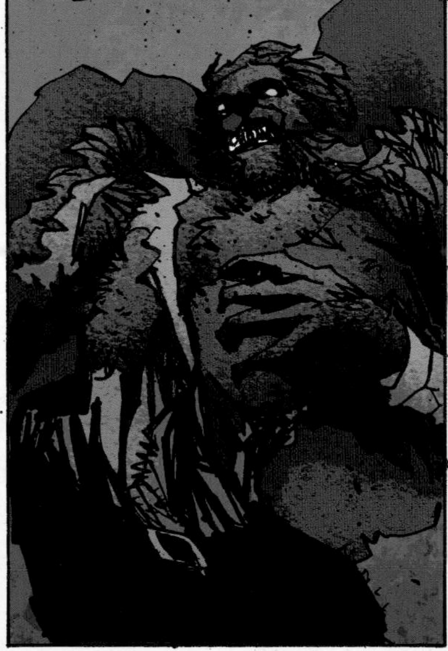

YOU KILLED HIM.
HE'S GONE?

THE SHERIFF? HOW DID YOU KNOW...?
MERLIN HATED HIM. AND MERLIN'S ALWAYS HATED DOGS. BESIDES... THE MAYOR WAS DEFINITELY NOT AN ALPHA.

YOU LET HIM INFECT YOUR SON.

SHERIFF POWELL WAS THREATENED BY MY POSITION IN TOWN. HE DEMANDED A SHOW OF LOYALTY. HE DEMANDED MY SON.
AND WHEN I GAVE HIM TO HIM, HE SLASHED HIM. INFECTED HIM. SAID MY SON WAS NOW HIS.

GO HOME. THE BONDS HAVE BEEN BROKEN. YOU'RE FREE NOW.

I DON'T KNOW... I'M BETTING THE MAYOR'S NEVER GOING TO BE FREE.

PORTLAND, MAINE.
LOOKS LIKE YOU'RE IN THE CLEAR.
I THINK WE'LL WANT TO CONTINUE THESE INJECTIONS FOR A WHILE, BUT YOUR LAST BLOOD WORK CAME BACK *CLEAN*.
THE SILVER ANTIBIOTIC DESTROYED THE VIRUS AS WE HYPOTHESIZED.
AFTER REBECCA DIED AND MY LICENSE WAS REVOKED, I ATTEMPTED SUICIDE.
REBECCA... *STOPPED* ME. SHE *SAVED* ME.
LUCKY FOR ME, I GUESS.

DR. HORNE'S CURE WORKED FINE ON DETECTIVE HUFFMAN, BUT WE WERE LESS FORTUNATE WITH JENNA WALSH. THE INFECTION WAS TOO FAR ALONG.
THERE IS FEAR THAT INTRODUCING THE SILVER COMPOUND WOULD CAUSE CASCADING SYSTEM FAILURE.

NICE WORK, DR. HORNE. DR. TEAGUE TELLS ME THE TESTS HAVE CONFIRMED THE SHERIFF WAS THE ONLY PERSON IN TOWN INFECTED. LOOKS LIKE WE'RE DONE HERE.
GLAD TO SEE YOU'RE WELL, DETECTIVE HUFFMAN.
WHAT'S GOING TO HAPPEN TO JENNA WALSH?

THE C.D.C. WILL PUT TOGETHER A TEAM TO WORK ON A LONG-TERM CURE. MEANWHILE, WE'LL KEEP JENNA UNDER OBSERVATION.

EXCUSE ME, DEPUTY DIRECTOR? BUT YOUR ORGANIZATION CONFISCATED A VIDEOTAPE FROM A LOCAL POLICE OFFICER.
HE *REALLY* NEEDS THAT TAPE BACK SO THAT HE CAN BE CLEARED OF THE SHOOTING.

ALRIGHT.
BUT YOU NEED TO DO SOMETHING FOR ME.

I'D LIKE TO MAKE THIS TEAM *PERMANENT*.
WITH YOU IN CHARGE, DR. HORNE.

CONGRATS, DOC! I THINK SHE LIKES YOU.
HMPH.

WE NEEDED JAMES. SOMEONE WHO WAS GOOD WITH THE PATIENTS.
YOU'RE NOT... ALL BAD.

THANKS, BUT...
...I HAVE ANOTHER IDEA.

DR. ANDERSON? IF YOU HAVE A MINUTE...

✚ NUNZIO DEFILIPPIS & CHRISTINA WEIR

Nunzio DeFilippis and Christina Weir are a writing team trained as screenwriters. They have worked in television, on and off, for the last fifteen years. They were on the writing staff of HBO's *Arliss* for two seasons, and worked on Disney's *Kim Possible*. They have also written an independent film called *Paradise Springs* that is in development.

In comics, they have primarily made their home at Oni Press, who have let them write books in a wide array of genres, including *Skinwalker*, *Three Strikes*, *Maria's Wedding*, *Past Lies*, *The Tomb*, *Frenemy of the State*, and *The Amy Devlin Mysteries*.

They have also written superhero comics like *New Mutants*, *New X-Men*, *Adventures of Superman*, and *Batman Confidential*, and have worked in the field of manga, adapting numerous series for Del Rey. They created three Original English Language Manga series for Seven Seas Entertainment: *Amazing Agent Luna*, *Dracula Everlasting*, and *Destiny's Hand*, with a two-volume Luna spinoff called *Amazing Agent Jennifer*.

In 2012, Nunzio and Christina released *The Avalon Chronicles* with Emma Vieceli and *Play Ball* illustrated by Jackie Lewis as well as *Bad Medicine*, all published by Oni Press. They also just completed their first prose novel, a young adult thriller called *Mind Dance*, and are at work writing a second novel and a new screenplay.

✚ CHRISTOPHER MITTEN

Originally from the cow-dappled expanse of southern Wisconsin, Christopher Mitten now spends his time roaming the misty wilds of suburban Chicago, drawing little people in little boxes.

In addition to Oni Press, he has contributed work for Dark Horse, DC Comics, Wildstorm, IDW, 44FLOOD, Image, and Simon & Schuster.

He can be found online at *christophermitten.com* and followed on Twitter. *twitter.com/chris_mitten*.

✚ BILL CRABTREE

Bill Crabtree's career as a colorist began in 2003 with *Invincible* and *Firebreather*, published by Image Comics. His work on *Invincible* was Harvey Awards nominated, and he went on to color the first 50 issues of what would become a flagship Image Comics title. He continues to color *Firebreather*, which was recently made into a feature film on Cartoon Network, *Godland*, and *Jack Staff*, as well as the Oni Press series *The Sixth Gun*, for which he was nominated for an Eisner Award in 2012.